RENEWALS 458-4574
DATE DUE

WITHDRAWN
UTSA LIBRARIES

Gramsci, Migration, and the Representation of Women's Work in Italy and the U.S.

Gramsci, Migration, and the Representation of Women's Work in Italy and the U.S.

Laura E. Ruberto

LEXINGTON BOOKS

A DIVISION OF
ROWMAN & LITTLEFIELD PUBLISHERS, INC.
Lanham • Boulder • New York • Toronto • Plymouth, UK

LEXINGTON BOOKS

A division of Rowman & Littlefield Publishers, Inc.
A wholly owned subsidiary of The Rowman & Littlefield Publishing Group, Inc.
4501 Forbes Boulevard, Suite 200
Lanham, MD 20706

Estover Road
Plymouth PL6 7PY
United Kingdom

Copyright © 2007 by Lexington Books

All rights reserved. No part of this publication may be reproduced,
stored in a retrieval system, or transmitted in any form or by any
means, electronic, mechanical, photocopying, recording, or otherwise,
without the prior permission of the publisher.

British Library Cataloguing in Publication Information Available

Library of Congress Cataloging-in-Publication Data

Ruberto, Laura E.
  Gramsci, migration, and the representation of women's work in Italy and the U.S. /
Laura E. Ruberto.
    p. cm.
  Includes bibliographical references and index.
  ISBN-13: 978-0-7391-1073-7 (cloth : alk. paper)
  ISBN-10: 0-7391-1073-X (cloth : alk. paper)
  1. Women—Employment—Italy. 2. Women—Italy—Social conditions. 3. Italian
American women—Employment. 4. Gramsci, Antonio, 1891–1937—Criticism and
interpretation. I. Title.
  HD6154.R83 2007
  331.4086'9120973—dc22   2007006359

Printed in the United States of America

∞™ The paper used in this publication meets the minimum requirements of
American National Standard for Information Sciences—Permanence of Paper
for Printed Library Materials, ANSI/NISO Z39.48-1992.

Ai miei genitori

Contents

	Acknowledgments	ix
Introduction	Women Workers, Migration, and a Gramscian Perspective	1
Chapter 1	Italian Rice Workers and National Popular Culture	33
Chapter 2	Migrant Domestic Labor and the Creation of Identity	51
Chapter 3	Work and the Italian American Home in Cinema	81
Chapter 4	"All Colors, All Religions, All United": Women Workers in California's Canneries	109
Epilogue	After Modotti	123
	Bibliography	127
	Index	139
	About the Author	149

Acknowledgments

This book has taken many years to complete and along the way I have been influenced by countless teachers, colleagues, students, family members, and friends. I hope they all see their impact in these pages.

I would like to acknowledge Robert Carley at Lexington for first approaching me about my dissertation, as well as many others at Lexington/Rowman and Littlefield for remaining committed to my project as I worked on revising the book.

The earliest stages of this book were written while I was a graduate student in the Department of Literature at the University of California at San Diego. As such, the project benefited much from the guidance and intellectual rigor of many, including Stephanie Jed, Pasquale Verdicchio, Lisa Lowe, Pamela Radcliff, and Oumelbene Zhiri. Similarly, Kristi M. Wilson, Grace Kyungwon Hong, Demian Pritchard, and Anupama Taranath were influential in helping me complete what became the complete first draft of this study, my dissertation.

While in graduate school I spent extensive time in Bologna, performing archival research on Renata Viganò and the *mondine*; I combed the archives of the Istituto Gramsci Emilia-Romagna, the Centro di documentazione delle donne, the Cineteca di Bologna, and the Associazione Nazionale Partigiani d'Italia (ANPI). Various members of the University of Bologna's *Gruppo di ricerca su donne e resistenza* were very helpful in this time period. Likewise, my volunteer work with the Support Committee for Maquiladora

Workers in San Diego came at a pivotal time in my studies. These varied experiences were invaluable to my entire project.

Since graduate school many colleagues and friends have continued to help shape the book. Pasquale Verdicchio and Stephanie Jed further guided my project as it moved from dissertation to manuscript. Similarly, Deborah Gilbert, Kristi M. Wilson, and Matthew Mulligan Goldstein commented on versions of this book numerous times. Different types of support have also come from Teri Ann Bengiveno, Jonathan Blum, Mary Jo Bona, George Boulukos, JoAnn Cannon, Clarissa Clò, Anna Collette, Tomàs F. Crowder-Taraborrelli, Steven P. Devine, Dina Fachin, Teresa Fiore, Fred L. Gardaphè, Jennifer Mulligan Goldstein, Michael Henry, Margherita Heyer-Caput, Maria Kotsaftis, Staci Markos, Bettina Moore, Marcelo Paz, Joseph Sciorra, Paola Sensi-Isolani, Anthony Julian Tamburri, and Elizabeth Wing-Paz.

I wish to express particular gratitude to my family, those who have always had confidence in my intellectual pursuits. My parents, Anna Ruberto and Raffaele G. Ruberto, and my brother and sister, Fabio D. Ruberto and Beatrice I. Ruberto, have supported all I do since before I learned to say "I can swim." I also thank Beatrice Ruberto and Ernestine Ruberto Franco for copyediting the manuscript. Much needed and much appreciated encouragement has come from other extended family across two continents, including members of the Goldstein, Ruberto, De Pedis, and Conte families.

My greatest debt goes to Matthew, whose affection, companionship, and constant encouragement led to the completion of this book. And finally, I thank Dante, whose language games always make me smile and Alma, who arrived just in time.

This book incorporates elements of previously published material, work found in *Italian Americana: Cultural and Historical Review* (Summer 2003) and *Perspectives on Italian and Italian American Women* (2003).

INTRODUCTION

Women Workers, Migration, and a Gramscian Perspective

> We cannot write women into history, for example, unless we are willing to entertain the notion that history as a unified story was a fiction about a universal subject whose universality was achieved through implicit processes of differentiation, marginalization, and exclusion.
>
> —Joan Scott, *Gender and the Politics of History*, 197

Both Cesare Pavese's novella "Tra donne sole" ("Among Women Alone") and Michelangelo Antonioni's screen version of the story, *Le amiche* (*Girlfriends*), explore the relationship of a group of middle-class women in post–World War II Turin. In both the written and cinematic versions, labor signifies independence and a mode of expression for Italian bourgeois women. Most of the female characters do not work for a living, but the two who do, Clelia and Nene, are emotionally invested in their work. Labor for these women represents free will, independence, happiness, and, most importantly, a medium for self-expression. For all the women, though, employment, or the lack of it, influences their life decisions. In Pavese's version, Rosetta, who lives *la dolce vita*, recognizes the uselessness of her bourgeois life and, unable to change, commits suicide. In the film version, Clelia, a successful businesswoman, decides she must break up with her lover, Carlo, in order to follow her career as an atelier owner. Clelia, who worked her way up from a working-class background, defines herself and her way of being via her relationship to labor. She explains this relationship to Carlo: "Working is also my way of being a woman, of loving, of participating in life, do you understand?"[1] She tells him she must leave Turin and return to Rome, because if she were to stay with him she would take up a more traditional housewife role and in so doing hopelessly compromise her identity.

Clelia's statement shows us a useful way to think about women and work in the Italian context. Her statement, representing the significance labor has in the formation of personal identity, will serve as a point of departure for the discussion in the following pages of representations of other groups of women workers. First, however, we must complicate the definition of labor Clelia's statement offers by showing how the pressures exerted by such forces as class, race, and national identity, when examined alongside gender, disrupt so apparently liberating a definition of work. Through close readings of a variety of cultural representations of laboring migrant women, I hope to point out some of the limits that inhere in the dominant narratives of postunification Italian history, including those bearing on the history of Italians in the United States; such attention to those we might term the representationally underconsidered makes possible a sharper critical understanding of the ways in which dominant culture has been formed discursively throughout the twentieth century.

It is not hard to see that labor and a celebration of labor were at the heart of post–World War II Italian culture. Perhaps the Italian constitution (written in 1946) best illustrates this position. Its first line, "L'Italia è una Repubblica democratica fondata sul lavoro" ("Italy is a democratic Republic founded on labor"), opens a document that has been celebrated as one of the most progressive constitutions for its support of workers' rights. Focusing on the labor of migrant women within an Italian context and questioning received notions about what work is and who performs it can, perhaps, complicate this celebration.[2] This critique of identity in relation to labor will come out of close readings of a variety of interrelated textual representations. The textual examples under consideration include films, novels, short stories, songs, recipes, and testimonials. The examples will take us from photographs of San Diego's canning industry to songs about rice workers in Emilia-Romagna, from Italo-African oral testimonies to Italian American women in film and beyond. By looking at such varied representations of women workers I hope to show the multiplicity of their histories. That is, in order to "write women into history" (Scott 197), we must consider all types of cultural productions in which women have been represented (or have represented themselves). Such a critical consideration of a variety of textual representations takes to task the traditional idea of "history as a unified story" (Scott

197) by pointing to the moments where this supposedly complete history was created and upheld at the expense of marginalized and repressed voices.

The Italian Marxist thinker and political activist Antonio Gramsci is a key character in my present conceptualization of women's migratory labor. Mine is not a historical study but a cultural one. The emphasis here is on what representation reveals about cultural and political change. With this in mind, Gramsci's thoughts on national popular culture, the social role of subalterns and organic intellectuals, the politics of folklore (or "common sense") and everyday culture, and the need to build alliances across multiple directions all act as central unifying theories. Such theories, when refashioned with a feminist perspective in mind, further strengthen their original purpose.

As such, this chapter outlines the theoretical basis for the book as a whole: first, reviewing certain aspects of the field of labor history, then introducing some of Gramsci's concepts most pertinent to the present study, and, finally, arguing for a broad and nuanced understanding of the relationship between women, labor, and migration in an Italian context.

The role of migration is particularly important to keep in mind as other theoretical models are introduced. The representations of working women considered in the subsequent chapters all have some kind of relationship to the geo-political area known today as Italy—either the women were born and lived in Italy, or they (or their relatives) emigrated from Italy, or they (or their relatives) immigrated to Italy. I purposely wish to see these different kinds of movements as related to and reflective of one another.

A location such as Italy offers a complex and productive space within which to study the intersections of migration, gender, and culture. Italy's own history of emigration and expansive diasporic communities, coupled with the rhetorical history of the peninsula as both a romantic, historical, tourist attraction, and, simultaneously, not quite a First World nation marks it as unique. In short, the monolithic First World is broken apart when looking at the southern European peninsula of Italy.[3] This understanding of migration, introduced in more depth at the end of this chapter, remains the basic structuring principle for the analyses I take up throughout the book.

Further, Italy's unique history of emigration/immigration/internal migration can be used as a model for cultural interventions on the topics of women, labor, and migration generally. Critical insights about race and ethnicity are as important to an understanding of internal migration within postwar Italy as they are to an understanding of Italian emigration to North America and of recent immigration from North Africa, Central Europe, and Southeast Asia to Italy. In each case, as the following chapters highlight, details such as an individual's race, class, or cultural background greatly influence how that person will be accepted (or not) by his or her newly adopted country/region. Weaving this complex idea of migration into a consideration of culture and labor can lead us to plot the different forces at play in the representation of women; for what links all of the women under consideration here is their position (however varied) as migrants. Such a study, then, can point toward a revisited historical discourse as well as a critical approach to the contemporary development of the European Union, the position of ethnicity and race in the United States, and globalization in general.

Where Labor Histories Stand

Traditional Marxism describes historical development as the relationship between the owners of capital and the producers of capital. Marx emphasized the centrality of the male, urban factory worker, who is produced, in a continuous cycle, by the same capital he helps create. As a result, European and U.S. labor histories committed to Marxism for the most part do not discuss the situation of such gendered labor as rice work or domestic work. In fact, the majority of these analyses remain within the realm of the industrialized urban space: Even though they examine peasants and various agricultural workers, when it comes to discussing labor actions, historians' discourse tends to move out of the farms and into the factories.[4] While some Italian and U.S. labor histories recognize the existence of women factory workers, especially in time of war, labor regarded as women's work—in any location—is regularly not seen as being as historically significant as so-called men's work.[5] Even within urban-focused studies, work ordinarily performed by women, such as domestic labor (paid or unpaid), is not usually discussed in labor histories. In the late 1980s Joan Scott noted sarcastically that "[s]ome labor historians, acting on a kind of popular front mentality, now place gender (along with race) on the list of variables they acknowledge as important, but don't have time to study; class, after all, is still the issue that really counts" (54). Until the last few decades this approach to the history of labor meant that much of the labor of women, people of color, and immigrants was not seen to fit into the pre-existing materialist model of history, and, thus, these stories were marginalized, repressed, or forgotten. Commendable for their insistence on a class-based analysis of history, U.S. and Italian historical narratives about labor have come under attack in recent decades for their seeming blindness to other factors (race, gender, ethnicity, nationality, sexuality), which contribute to the material formations of the development of capitalism within and between nations.

Traditional labor histories often skip over many types of work. Simply put, these lapses might be divided into three somewhat overlapping categories of labor, all performed by women, people of color, and migrant groups generally: work that is unwaged, unorganized, or not carried out in a factory. The specific employment groups focused on in these pages fit into one or more of these gaps. Revisionist labor historians and cultural critics have taken up these various gaps often by looking to nontraditional historical documents, ephemera, vernacular culture, and creative works in order to trace histories of repression and hidden forms of resistance. One consequence, within an Italian context, of the development of such revisionist histories is that dominant ideas about Italian cultural and national identity are challenged and consequently changed to include the toils of these groups of workers. In short, long-accepted notions about history radically shift, as Joan Scott in the epigraph above aptly explains with respect to women and the past.

In the introduction to her edited collection, *Work Engendered*, Ava Baron concisely explains the movements over the last few decades within the very broad discipline of labor history and the ways in which U.S. labor histories (generally until the 1960s) focused "on formal institutions of power, on male leaders and their organizations, [and] virtually excluded women from considerations" (2). Then, continues Baron, the 1970s saw a shift to the study of union members and unorganized workers, a kind of "working class history," which more directly paved the way for studies of ethnic and immigrant groups, at least in the field of U.S. history (2–3). Yet, even though such studies opened up the exploration of women's history, a distinction remained firm: "working class history has remained a preserve of male workers" (Baron 4). In other words, scholars still often begin with the assumption that "workers" and "the working class" refer to men.

The theoretical assumptions that inevitably come from such an understanding of labor have to do with, for instance, ideas of historical periodization that usually "rel[y] on male experience and changes in men's status despite women's historians' persuasive arguments that traditional periodization has been gender-biased" (Baron 5). Perhaps the most appropriate example of how traditional periodization can cause gender biases has to do with labor during World War II. The war offered many European and U.S. women a chance to explore life outside the confines of their traditional domestic duties and traditional female forms of employment. Such opportunities, many scholars suggest, paved the way for the kinds of political and social liberations women in these countries enjoyed after the war (the best examples might be gaining the vote in countries like France and Italy). That a large-scale international catastrophe such as World War II might have been beneficial to a great number of women is a paradox that only feminists have explored. Thus Sherna Berger Gluck in her *Rosie the Riveter Revisited* concludes:

> The potential for social transformation was created by the wartime need for women workers. For a brief period, images of women were revised, employment opportunities were expanded, and public policy was enacted that created new services for women. These were necessary, but not sufficient conditions. Social values also had to change, including women's definitions of themselves. Women's wartime experiences played a vital role in that process of redefinition—the reverberations of which are still being felt today. (270)

While such scholarship around World War II helps alleviate the kinds of problems Baron outlines with respect to historical periodization, women remain often unnoticed within discussions of labor histories. Scott sees that "[m]ost [labor historians] ignore gender entirely, insisting either that it is absent from their sources or that (unfortunately) women played only a minor role in the working-class politics that mattered" (55). She argues for a scholarship that "attempts to bring women as a subject and gender as an analytical category into the practice of labor history" (53). Taking off from Scott's call for a more complex analysis, Baron concludes:

> Gender, then, is constituted through people's lived experience within continually redefined and contested social activities and institutions. Gender is integral not only to relations between men and women, but also to a myriad of other relations of power and hierarchy, including those between employers and workers, men and boys, whites and blacks. As a social process, we need to think of *gender* not only as a noun but also as a verb. The study of gendering is concerned with how understandings of sexual difference shape institutions, practices, and relationships. (36, emphasis in original)

The contemporary Italian association of feminist historians, *Le storiche*, echoes Baron's words. In speaking specifically about the case of the Italian anti-Fascist resistance, they point out how changing one's perspective can at once distort certain assumed facts and bring into focus new ones:

> Il riconoscimento delle donne come soggetti ed agenti di cambiamento—risultato ormai acquisito dagli studi di storia delle donne—ha significato scomporre un universo femminile, troppo spesso considerato indifferenziato, in una pluralità di percorsi biografici e richiamare l'attenzione sulla molteplicità delle esperienze, sulle somiglianze, ma anche sulle diversità legate alle appartenenze ideologiche e culturali alle provenienze sociali e geografiche, agli aspetti gen-

erazionali, al momento delle scelte individuali. (Gagliani, Guerra, Mariani, Tarozzi 1)

The recognition of women as subjects and agents of change—a result acquired by studies of women's histories—signifies regrouping a female universe, too often considered indistinct, into a plurality of biographical paths and it calls attention to a multiplicity of experiences, to similarities, but also to the differences which are all tied to ideological and cultural belonging, to various social and geographical sources, to generational aspects, and to the moment of individual choice.

For these historians, women's history involves more than adding the activities of women to a pre-existing narrative: They work toward highlighting the plurality of voices, the multiplicity of perspectives and experiences, and the different ways in which diversity is influenced by intersecting categories, or axes, of identification—such as culture, location, and generation. Part of this differentiation process entails incorporating, very explicitly, other categories of identification such as race and ethnicity. Extending *Le storiche*'s proposal means recognizing that *gender*—as a theoretical category that refers generically to *women* or as a category infused with real and theoretical power struggles—does not sufficiently complicate materialist-based ideas of labor and class. As Chandra Talpade Mohanty's influential piece "Under Western Eyes" reminds us, the concept of woman must always be differentiated to include other categories of identification, such as race, class, and ethnicity.[6]

An example of a historical study that acknowledges complexities related to identity formation and the production of historical discourse can be found in Elizabeth Ewen's *Immigrant Women in the Land of Dollars*, a study of Jewish and Italian immigrant women workers in New York. In her introduction, Ewen locates herself outside of the trend of social historians who see the significance of studying immigrant ethnic cultural traditions solely in explorations of the "Americanization" of ethnic communities and their relationship to the economy. She extends such study of economic mobilization to women and children: "While ethnic history is, as historian Herbert Gutman has noted, labor—and therefore class—history, class does not end at the factory gate: working class history is shaped by a totality of experiences . . ." (14).[7] Her focus on gender and ethnicity within a study of class points out the shortcomings of traditional labor histories and laments their lack of engagement with such issues.

Ewen's study is part of an ever-growing body of critical work that points out the blind spots in traditional labor histories with respect to race and ethnicity. Even though race is now commonly considered in labor histories, more recent work examines the sometimes troubling ways in which race gets addressed within class discussions.[8] As David R. Roediger in his *Wages of Whiteness* explains, this position sets out to show how "the privileging of class over race is not always productive or meaningful. To set race within social formations is absolutely necessary, but to reduce race to class is damaging" (8). In other words, a traditional Marxist perspective applied to issues of race and ethnicity sees these categories as dependent on the economic structures of society and thereby subordinates race to class.[9]

For traditional (and not so traditional) Marxists, sociocultural reform is supposed to evolve naturally after economic reform—a very nebulous structure, to say the least—which downplays other factors such as gender and race. These absences in Marxist thought can be seen to parallel U.S. and European labor histories' general disregard for women migrant workers and further suggest why we must turn to nontraditional forms of historical documentation (such as films, testimonials, songs, and vernacular culture) and to renegotiations of materialism and feminism if we are to understand the place of women workers in the fabric of cultural history.

Gramsci: Toward a Working Theory

Antonio Gramsci's historical analysis reconfigured Marx's work by, among other things, asserting the ongoing importance of the peasantry within the traditional socialist narrative of development and insisting on the need for alliances between different types of workers in order to achieve successful political and cultural revolution. Furthermore, many of his perspectives are useful for analyzing the role that gender, class, and race play in the formation of identities and the way cultural representations encourage and sustain certain social power structures.

Gramsci's contributions to radical political philosophy were not altogether unexpected, given the intellectual promise he showed from a young age. Born in 1891 in Cagliari (in the province of Sardegna), Gramsci won a university scholarship for students of limited economic means. He left for Turin, Italy's industrial center, where his studies focused mainly on linguistics and social science. By 1915 he had joined the Italian Socialist Party and had left university life in order to pursue full-time work as a political activist, journalist, and public speaker. Inspired by the Bolshevik revolution and other global political changes, he helped found the Italian Communist Party in 1921 and its daily news organ *L'Unità* in 1924. Fellow Socialist Benito Mussolini organized his own political group, the *Fasci di combattimento*, in the same period and by 1922 was dictator of Italy and the leader of the newly formed Fascist Party. By 1926, Mussolini had imprisoned many of his enemies, among them Gramsci, who was already well known in intellectual circles for his fiery essays, including those that treated the so-called Southern Question (in which he posited the potential to organize northern factory workers with southern peasants). Mussolini made Gramsci's political activism more difficult by imprisonment but not impossible, and he went on to write some of his most influential works from his cell. (He died in prison in 1937.) By the early 1950s both his *Lettere dal carcere* (*Letters from Prison*) and *Quaderni dal carcere* (*Prison Notebooks*) were published, first incompletely and only in Italian.

Although unfinished, Gramsci's writings are important to a discussion of women and labor, especially as they relate to migration. His understanding of a class-based national popular culture founded on alliances between different subaltern classes (sometimes with the help of an organic intellectual) and his privileging of everyday practices and what he called "folklore" are all relevant here. For Gramsci, understanding society through the perspective of the subaltern is fundamental. The subaltern is a specific term Gramsci borrowed from British military terminology that for him incorporates all politically and culturally disenfranchised people (including but not limited to women). Simply put, the positive value he placed on culture produced by the subaltern classes helps underscore the position women (both as historical beings and as representations) hold with respect to the formation of culture. Feminists have long understood Gramsci's usefulness to a gender-nuanced theory. As Lucia Chiavola Birnbaum describes with respect to the Italian feminist group Rivolta femminile: "They are indebted to Gramsci's emphasis on cultural revolution, the revolution as a dialectical process, the importance of regional differences (particularly the cultural and economic difference of the South), the significance of self-confidence in socialist self-management, and careful strategy in periods of backlash" (29). Nevertheless the group also notes the limitations Gramsci's writings have with respect to a discussion of sexuality, women, and relations of power.

It does not take much for us to find practical examples of such limitations. For example, even when Gramsci used examples from Italy's recent past to illustrate his thoughts on revolution, he excluded the participation of women. In his preprison article "Some Notes on the Southern Question" (commonly published as *The Southern Question*), he explains that for a revolution to be successful, the proletariat must unite with peasants (in this case he refers to northern workers and southern peasants):

> That, in addition to overcoming distinctions that exist between one trade and another, it is necessary [for the proletariat], in order to win the trust and consensus of the peasants and of some semi-proletarian categories within the

cities, to overcome certain prejudices and conquer certain forms of egoism which can and do subsist within the working class . . . (27)

Recognizing differences and then deciding to form alliances based on a common struggle is Gramsci's effective strategy. In *The Southern Question*, Gramsci refers to Red Week as an example of a successful mass labor action that took place among northern peasants and factory workers. Curiously enough, according to Elda Gentili Zappi, the *mondine* (Italian female rice workers) were central figures in its success, yet Gramsci does not mention the women—a small but severe omission whereby Gramsci leaves migrant women out of the alliance-making process.[10] Thus although Gramsci noted the benefit of uniting different repressed groups in order to form a successful cultural hegemony, he nonetheless overlooks the impact of female migrant labor.

Nonetheless, to mention Gramsci and feminist issues in the same breath is not particularly shocking either; Teresa de Lauretis, Renate Holub, Marcia Landy, Anne Showstack Sasson, the Rivolta femminile group, and others have long examined how Gramsci, the philosopher, complicated the Marxist Woman Question by recognizing the role of sexuality in the production of capital and culture. At the same time, they realize that Gramsci, the man, fell short in his application of feminism in his interaction with women, and they point to the ways in which dominant historical narratives failed to recognize the influence of women on Gramsci. By looking at the different ways Gramsci's thoughts on the Woman Question have been critiqued by contemporary feminists, I hope to move beyond the Gramscian Woman Question by extending it through a focus on migration, globalization, and the fragmentation and representation of identity.

It is only because of the work of feminists that Gramsci's wife, Julia Schucht, and in particular his sister-in-law, Tatiana Schucht, have been recognized for the moral and personal support they offered him while in prison, support that invigorated him enough to write some of the most important Marxist pieces of the last century. Late twentieth-century feminist analysis has clarified the role of the Schucht sisters in Gramsci's prison writing. Since Fascist law for the most part only permitted Gramsci to correspond with relatives while he was incarcerated, his party friends, like Piero Sraffa, had to rely in great measure on Tatiana to relay messages to Gramsci through her letters. And it was Tatiana (who was living in Italy, rather than Julia, who was in the Soviet Union) who saved Gramsci's writings and letters after his death. In fact de Lauretis discusses Gramsci and his position on women by studying the letters Tatiana and Julia wrote *to* him. These letters remained collecting dust in the Gramsci Institute in Rome until, in 1975, the Italian feminist group *La Maddalena* performed a play, *Nonostante Gramsci* (*Gramsci Notwithstanding*), collectively written about the then-unpublished letters from Julia Schucht and Tatiana Schucht. De Lauretis notes how the play (both as a written text and as performance) writes a new history, a feminist conception of the relation between Gramsci and some of the women in his life. Working within their own brand of second-wave feminism, the women behind the play were able to create a woman-centered space and retrieve a previously hidden piece of the past.

Holub, meanwhile, looks at the letters Gramsci wrote to Julia and Tatiana as a way of engaging with Gramsci, the intellectual. As she reminds us: "It should be pointed out that Gramsci was not particularly well versed in the issues of feminism of his time, at least not more, but also not less, than most of those of his contemporaries whose chosen business was to deal with issues of political and economic equality and justice" (195). Holub uses these letters and the relationship between Gramsci and the Schucht sisters as an entry into a broader discussion of Gramsci and gender. In a similar vein, Mimma Paulesu's little-known historical text, *Le donne di casa Gramsci* (*The Women of Gramsci's Home*), traces the lives of the women in Gramsci's family in Sardegna and suggests that his family and his female relatives in particular were central in the formation and development of his theories. She recounts the lives of Emma and Teresina, Gramsci's sisters who both held jobs and participated in labor strikes, and Peppina, a third sister who co-founded one of the first women's social organizations on the island, the *Circolo femminile*, in Gramsci's home town of Ghilarza. While Gramsci lived in Turin and the Soviet Union, and later while he was in prison in Rome and Turi (in the province of Bari), they were crucial in keeping him up-to-date on the political and cultural occurrences of his native Sardegna, situations that were no doubt important to Gramsci, as they reflected on questions of national unity and cultural strife he often pondered in his writings.

Looking at some of Gramsci's letters to Julia and Tatiana, we can see very quickly what Holub describes as the "harsh, authoritarian and condescending" tone he takes toward both sisters (194).[11] In April 1927, six months into his ten-year incarceration, he reprimands Tatiana for not sending him Julia's letters more quickly, and he offers his thoughts on women's nature:

> Tu, come tutte le donne in generale, hai molta immaginazione e poca fantasia e ancora, l'immaginazione in te (come nelle donne in generale) lavora in un solo senso, nel senso che io chiamerei (ti vedo fare un salto) . . . protettore degli animali, vegetariano, infermieristico: le donne sono liriche (per elevarci un po') ma non sono drammatiche. (Gramsci, *Lettere* 52)

> You, like all women in general, have a lot of imagination but little fantasy and still, the imagination you have (like in women in general) works in only one way, in the sense that I will call (I see you flinch) . . . protector of animals, vegetarian, nurse-like: women are lyrical (to raise us up a bit) but they are not dramatic.

Here he appears to understand women as possessing only typical maternal qualities, which are almost expressly meant to benefit "us," men. In addition, he suggests an almost John Locke-style distinction between ideas and knowledge when he states that women have the possibility to imagine but not to fantasize (the possibility to think but not to create, perhaps?).

On the other hand, a gentler, more sensible Gramsci comes through in other instances, and we can also extract part of his theory from his own biography. In the following example we can see, in fact, how he may have begun formulating ideas he later outlined in the "Americanism and Fordism" section of the *Prison Notebooks*. In January of 1931 he writes to Julia that he does not think they have been honest to each other, and that they should try to treat each other more like equals and partners:

> Perché non abbiamo mantenuto la parola? Perché non rompiamo assolutamento con questi modi di condotta che sentono di vita feudale, di Domostroi, di legislazione inglese del 700? (secondo questa legislazione il marito nascondeva alla moglie la vita dei figli e i tribunali sanzionavano che tra madre e figlio non esisteva parentela!). (*Lettere* 141)[12]

> Why didn't we keep our word? Why don't we completely break from these ways of acting which are practically feudal, of the Domostroi, like British legislation from the 1700s? (according to this law the husband hid the children from his wife, and the court sanctioned that there was no relationship between mother and child!)

His desire for a new kind of masculine and feminine character comes through here, especially when we read this section alongside the next letter and his notes on sexuality in the *Notebooks*. In the next letter to Julia (February 1931) Gramsci, in a moment of crisis, spills out his emotions and again blames himself for their communication problems. He admits that he had held Julia too high on a pedestal, seeing her sometimes as only a "strong woman" and other times only as a weak woman needing to be fathered. He now takes a more even-handed position, realizing that she can be both weak and strong, that she is "insomma una donna viva, che [è] Iulca" ("in short a woman who is alive, that she [is] Julia") (142). He continues, acknowledging that he had seen himself as better than her but now realizes that, if anything, he is weaker than she (143).

In his letter to Julia he took some of the blame, and, in effect, suggested that he too must change and become a "new man" of sorts; however, in his notebooks, he mostly emphasizes changes in the way women view themselves (versus how others view them). In the section "Some aspects of the sexual question" (in the "Americanism and Fordism" section of the *Notebooks*), Gramsci speaks about a "new man" and a "new woman" in a study of U.S. manufacturing and production technology.[13] He recognizes that until a "new woman" exists, all forms of discipline and control of the sexuality of the workers attempted by management will be ineffectual:

> Finché la donna non avrà raggiunto non solo una reale indipendenza di fronte all'uomo, ma anche un nuovo modo di concepire se stessa e la sua parte nei rapporti sessuali, la questione sessuale rimarrà ricca di caratteri morbosi e occurrerà esser cauti in ogni innovazione legislativa. (*Note sul Machiavelli* 457)

> Until women have not reached a single real independence with respect to men, but also a new way of thinking about themselves and their part in sexual relationships, the sexual question will remain full of unhealthy characteristics, and we should be cautious in each legislative innovation.

This statement illustrates Gramsci's post-Marxist thinking. That is, Gramsci brings to the economic question the notion that the base is not the sole determinate of social and cultural relationships: Rather, that the Fordist model of management, however hostile to labor, depends on an acknowledgment of the power of sexuality. His discussions of Americanism, and Fordism (and also Taylorism) seem to be both a critique of modernism and capitalism and a study of what Landy calls the "transformative potential" of certain aspects of modernity (227). He seems at once fascinated and disgusted with Ford's methods for improving production.

While the "new woman" must find it in herself to become a "woman who is alive" (*Lettere dal carcere* 142), a "new man" can only come about when the sexual instinct has been rationalized (by the demands of production). As Gramsci concludes: "Non può svilupparsi il nuovo tipo di uomo domandato dalla razionalizzazione della produzione e del lavoro, finché l'istinto sessuale non sia stato . . . regolato . . . e razionalizzato" ("The new type of man, compelled by the rationalization of production and of labor, cannot develop until the sexual instinct has been regulated and rationalized") (*Note sul Machiavelli* 457–458). Furthermore, Gramsci recognizes the possibility that this regulation (in the form of pro-family incentives, for instance) will one day be systematically imposed by the civic structure of a nation.[14] Landy sees in

Gramsci's description of a new man, "a worker whom [Gramsci] identifies in complex terms as involving heretofore unknown psychic, social, and political elements" (Landy 227). She ends her discussion of Americanism and Fordism admitting that some of his notes are puzzling, but confident that his ideas point toward useful practices for us today:

> Although Gramsci's comments are quite brief and cryptic and though one may question the basis of some of his generalizations about sexuality, in the larger picture it is clear that he understands that sexuality has become a force to be acknowledged and examined in relation to issues of coercion and consent. . . . The question of sexuality raises broader questions about the ways in which notions of public and private have been co-constituted, albeit they have been conceived in common sense terms as separate spheres in the interests of "laissez faire capitalism." (Landy 230)

Thus what we can take away from Gramsci's thinking is that he does not look at the system of capitalism solely within economic or political terms but rather complicates it with a look at the Woman Question, which is itself complicated by other factors, such as sexual reproduction. That his efforts still come up short by today's standards should not be taken to mean that we cannot gain from his insight or that we cannot use him as a starting point for development. As Holub points out, "[Sexuality] allows him not only to assess women's unequal status in our societies in terms of their economic exploitation and political marginalization from the public sphere, but also to point to women's material and symbolic function in the reproduction of the workforce necessary for production processes as a whole" (196). Holub suggests that what might have led Gramsci to an examination of women and sexuality is his interest in power relations and the notion of consent within civil structures such as schools, factories, and the family. In other words, Gramsci's study of hegemony, which depends on an understanding of consent as central to political control and revolution, led him to such a study of relations of power in everyday life.[15] It is in this sense, as Sasson also suggests, that "Gramsci can stand as the forerunner of the famous dictum of second-wave feminism: the personal is political" because he recognizes the force behind actions within the home and other conventional feminine spaces (Holub 197).[16] This emphasis on everyday culture and practice, especially in relation to the development of a kind of counter-hegemony, is one way Gramsci is useful in discussing the representation of migrant women and work.

Moving in a slightly different vein, Landy's comment above about how Gramsci helps rethink the constitution of private and public spaces is in line with Sasson's observation that Gramsci recognizes spaces within which the subaltern can produce culture (Sasson 25). In other words, the specificities of daily life and aspects of vernacular culture are important to a thorough understanding of cultural hegemony and hidden forms of resistance; Sasson thus reasons that "the use of Gramsci's categories can enrichen [sic] a feminist analysis of the transformation in women's oppression and the revolutionary implications of their new social role in the home, the productive sphere, and in society at large" (xviii). The following readings of representations of working women call attention to women's participation in the formation of such counter-hegemonic culture; in addition, my analyses show how different people have been engaged with the possibility of creating a culture based in part on migrant women's labor. Gramsci helps us recognize that women can be producers of such culture, as Landy explains: "The subaltern is not a melodramatic victim of injustice but an integral element in the overall conditions of domination and of change" (77).[17] In other words, since for Gramsci the private is public, "even activities which are ostensibly private have a political meaning and therefore are in turn part of the provision of the conditions under which a dominant mode of production can exist and expand" (Sasson 115). For instance, in the reading of Renata Viganò's *Una storia di ragazze* in chapter two, such "private" matters as abortion and unwed motherhood become tools for understanding class differences. Similarly in chapter one, the collective potential of rice workers exemplifies some of the ways alliances can be made across different moments of resistance and different disenfranchised groups. In addition, Gramsci's gesture toward an analysis of the relationship between private domestic space and public market space informs my critique of paid domestic labor in Italy, the cinematic representation of Italian American domesticity, and U.S. immigrant cannery workers. My epilogue's discussion of the photographer Tina Modotti is likewise informed by Gramsci's perspectives on organic intellectuals and the role of cultural representation.

Moreover, chapter three's consideration of Italian American women examines, in part, how immigrants built their American cultural identity out of powerful noninstitutionalized, "Old World" ideas about everyday life. This attachment to "folklore" or "common sense" (as Gramsci might put it) marks these women as immigrants.[18] Although Gramsci's notes on common sense are disconnected and sometimes even contradictory, he talks about common sense as a kind of false consciousness of peasants who see the world only through the perspective of their provincial life, and he compares it to "good sense," a concept of the world which recognizes one's position in the world in relation to others.[19] However, Gramsci's well-known statement that "all men are philosophers" implies that a common-sense notion of the world (one that suggests the possibility of philosophy though not its necessity) is essentially complex since it makes possible a theoretical and abstract *Weltanschauung*. Landy interprets Gramsci's notes on "common sense" by seeing it as a way of experiencing the world based on "various strata of philosophy, religion, institutional practices, and individual experiences" (Landy 78). Thus, in some ways, common sense can lead toward the kind of political and cultural change for which Gramsci pushes. Therefore, cultural identities (such as those of many migrant women), which illuminate through the labor and practice of everyday life a common sense notion of the world, are "a means of negotiating lived, if disjointed and counterproductive, conditions endemic to one's social group" (Landy 79).

Studying how a group's folklore or examples of common sense have been represented might then allow us to see the revolutionary potential of that culture. In many instances, the key to recognizing such potential in common sense or folklore is the need for hindsight. Lisa Lowe, in a discussion of Asian American culture, explains that for Gramsci, subaltern "histories are fragmented, episodic, and identifiable only from a point of historical hindsight" (69). That the history of subaltern groups—including struggles for hegemony—is best perceived with such distancing "suggests," as Lowe determines, "that some of the most powerful practices may not always be the explicitly oppositional ones, may not be understood by contemporaries, and may be less overt and recognizable than others" (69). Thus, a study that researches those texts representing the labor of marginalized women and their survival strategies allows us, perhaps, to identify challenges to dominant notions of culture and history.[20]

Through studying everyday practices, as Landy suggests, perhaps we can uncover how counter-hegemonies develop:

> The Gramscian conception of folklore and common sense and its relation to hegemony has implications for rethinking the nature and meaning of subalternity, a repositioning of it away from melodramatic notions of oppressor and oppressed and toward a more complex understanding of how subalternity is implicated in existing social and cultural formations through mechanisms of coercion and . . . mechanisms of consent. (Landy 15)

Thinking along these lines, we can begin to understand the importance of underscoring marginalized histories of women migrant workers. As this book illustrates the *mondina* who, through her songs, links her labor protests to anti-Fascism, the domestic worker who attempts to form cross-class solidarities, and the housewife whose unpaid labor within the context of immigration marks her with a certain ethnicity, all inform how culture and identity is created and sustained.

Women Workers, Migration, and a Gramscian Perspective   17

More specifically still, Gramsci's notion of the "national popular,"[21] a term he used to describe culture (and a national identity) that came directly from the lives of the working and peasant classes, recognizes the role of representation in the formation of cultural and political currents.[22] He promoted the production of culture that came from the experiences of the working and peasant classes (so-called subalterns); such national popular culture would stand against culture from the dominant classes. He recognized an absence of such national popular culture in Italy, "E perché non esiste in Italia una letteratura 'nazionale'?" ("Why is there no 'national' literature in Italy?") he asks (*Letteratura* 123, *Selected* 366). The answer, for Gramsci, lies in part in the idea of the organic intellectual who can help produce such culture. Organic intellectuals (as opposed to traditional intellectuals) come from the subaltern classes and act as bridges between the subaltern and the dominant classes. Instead of ignoring or patronizing the subaltern (as traditional intellectuals tend to do), organic intellectuals, for Gramsci, fortify subalterns with the tools they need to create a national popular culture. The organic intellectual can succeed through a strategic use of language—in practice, by translating, in a sense, the dominate culture for the subaltern and vice a versa.

Gramsci understands the movement toward hegemony by a subaltern class as deeply connected to language and, in turn, to language's relationship to class and culture. He noted the way language and fluency of the dominant language allows for appropriation of culture and the possibility for a progressive cultural hegemony. Gramsci maintains that while all language has the roots necessary for a complete understanding of society, knowledge of the dominant language is necessary for a counter-hegemony:

> Ogni linguaggio contiene gli elementi di una concezione del mondo e di una cultura . . . [ma] chi parla solo il dialetto o comprende la lingua nazionale in gradi diversi, partecipa necessariamente di una intuizione del mondo piú o meno ristretta e provinciale, fossilizzata, anacronistica in confronto delle grandi correnti di pensiero che dominano la storia mondiale. (*Il materialismo* 5)

> Every language contains the elements of a conception of the world and of a culture . . . [but] someone who only speaks dialect, or understands the standard language incompletely, necessarily has an intuition of the world which is more or less limited and provincial, which is fossilized and anachronistic in relation to the major currents of thought which dominate world history. (*Reader* 325)

Although the two most likely did not know each other's work, the Russian philosopher Mikhail Bakhtin, a contemporary of Gramsci,[23] offers an intriguing articulation of the power of language. Bakhtin argues that any individual can appropriate different strata of language, or "speech genres," for different purposes; in an often-quoted phrase, he explains: "The word in language is half someone else's. It becomes 'one's own' only when the speaker populates it with his own intention, his own accent, when he appropriates the word, adapting it to his own semantic and expressive intention" (*Dialogic* 293).[24] Such appropriation, however, is not always easy: "And not all words for just anyone submit equally easily to this appropriation, to this seizure and transformation into private property: many words stubbornly resist, others remain alien, sound foreign in the mouth of the one who appropriated them and who now speaks them; they cannot be assimilated into his context and fall out of will of the speaker" (*Dialogic* 294).

Bakhtin continues by using the example of "an illiterate peasant, miles away from any urban center," who lives and works using a variety of languages ("the language and world of prayer, the language and world of song, the language and world of labor and everyday life," etc.) (*Dialogic* 296). These languages are similar to Gramsci's common sense. For Bakhtin, these languages can live together harmoniously until the peasant in effect gains class consciousness ("as soon as it becomes clear . . . that the ideological systems and approaches to the world that were indissolubly connected with these languages contradicted each other") then the peasant must "actively choose one's orientation among them" (*Dialogic* 296). It is at this moment that a new counter-hegemony is formed.

Gramsci's concept of language and society differs from that of Bakhtin, who only thinks of language relative to class. Although Bakhtin notes that speech genres differ, in part because of the "situation, social position, and personal interrelations of the participants in the communication" (*Speech Genres* 79), he does not go far in critiquing the monologic qualities of certain speech genres, qualities that interfere with certain speakers' abilities to communicate effectively. Gramsci, by contrast, emphasizes the relationship between language, the speaker, and the specific space/location of the speech act. Such an emphasis on location becomes particularly relevant to a discussion on migrant labor. Holub, in comparing the work of Gramsci with that of Voloshinov (who some scholars equate with Bakhtin)[25] explains:

> [For Gramsci] language is situated in specific locations in a geographic space which contributes to its hegemony, a space from which its power disseminates, its prestige radiates. . . . This position, the hegemonic position of a language or a dialect, determines the adaptation of that language by other people who speak different languages, different dialects, and hold different systems of belief. (Holub 140)

In analyzing Gramsci's writings on language, Holub concludes: "Language, in its form as a structure of values, and mediated by agents of the hegemonic class, can keep the subaltern social classes in check. Yet subaltern classes can invent new structures of value designed to subvert the hegemonic design" (116). Thus Gramsci's national popular culture (that is, a movement toward a counter-hegemony) is dependent on, among other things, a strategic use of language, often in relation to an organic intellectual (language here is used loosely to extend to other forms of representation as well).

Gramsci's writings, therefore, help us recognize ways otherwise disenfranchised women might produce culture outside of or against hegemonic culture—through everyday practices, folklore, language (with or without the help of an organic intellectual), and alliance-building. However, such a theory has limitations as well. In a sense his concept of national popular, a unifying theme in my present study, is more of a process rather than a goal. An "international popular" culture may be a more appropriate way to consider the term within the contemporary era. For instance, Timothy S. Murphy in his "Expanding the Area of Autonomy: Music, Culture, and Politics in the Italian Counter-Culture 1964–1977," discusses Italian progressive rock bands and focuses on the group Area, who called themselves an "international popular group." Murphy analyzes the group's "intentional pun" of Gramsci whereby Gramsci's term is broadened to lose its nationalist edge and instead "transcends parochialism of the nation-state by finding [culture] . . . at an international, multicultural, or even global level" (unpublished conference paper). Pasquale Verdicchio reaches a similar conclusion in his *Bound by Distance*. In Verdicchio's "new way of being Gramscian" he names an "inter/national-popular . . . which does not aim to unite all subaltern or nondominant cultures as one; rather it proposes to offer resistance to nationalized notions of culture that would deny diversity within their borders" (168). Such modifications of Gramsci's original ideas remain important to a consideration of migrant women's labor because they remind us of the changing cultural and political landscape that Gramsci could not have imagined.

Thus, as the landscape of a country changes (through political shifts, migratory patterns, and economic swings), so does the usefulness of any national popular culture. As one national popular culture is constructed, another disenfranchised group (Gramsci's subalterns) lines up to begin creating its own national popular culture. That is, Gramsci's view of national popular culture assumes a unifying nation under which individuals attempt to recognize themselves and at the same time legitimates the nation-state. Migrants by definition force a redefinition of what it means to belong to a particular nation and thus encourage us to think about the way culture is formed in relation to the nation-state.

A Few Words on Migration and Italy

Italy's history of migration is unique on the European front and, as mentioned earlier, is a relevant aspect of this current study. Millions of newly nationalized Italians emigrated in the nineteenth and early twentieth centuries.[26] The majority of Italian emigration occurred between 1880 and 1930, when over 17 million women, men, and children left Italy, either permanently or seasonally. Women generally did not emigrate out of Italy alone but rather followed fathers, husbands, or brothers. When women did emigrate by themselves, they tended to move internally—to work, in the city, as domestic laborers or in factories, or as seasonal agricultural laborers, rice weeding or wheat harvesting.

Di Scala summarizes the strongest trends in Italian emigration as such: "Before the 1870s it had been seasonal, directed toward Europe, and involved the entire country; afterward, it became southern and permanent and had the Americas as its focus" (141). While most emigrated to the United States, predominant numbers also tried their luck in Australia, Canada, and countries in South America (mainly Brazil and Argentina). Although the majority of these emigrants left Italy permanently, some seasonal migration took place (so-called "birds of passage") even to places as far as the Americas. Moreover, a kind of internal migration, both seasonal and permanent, occurred. This migration grew alongside the development of factories in northern Italian cities, such as Turin and Milan, and brought people from the southern regions, the islands, and also some poorer northern regions (such as the Veneto) to urban areas looking for a way to make a living. Internal migration was not as easy for migrants as one might think since regional languages and cultures differed immensely and racism existed (and still exists) against southern Italians by their northern compatriots. In the post–World War II reconstruction period, Italians once again left their hometowns for work elsewhere; this was a smaller wave but one that nonetheless impacted both Italy and the Italian diaspora generally. Just as before, both seasonal and temporary migration occurred (both internally and to other countries), until the so-called economic miracle stabilized the economy, slowing down the movement of people.[27]

Today emigration and internal migration continues; however, Italy is now also home to what the Italian government and the media usually call *extracomunitari,* referring to immigrants from outside of the European Union. Most new immigrants originate from countries in Africa and Eastern Europe. In 1994 there were a little under 700,000 documented immigrant residents in Italy, today there are over 3 million. The number of immigrants residing in Italy is most likely much higher, due to undocumented immigrants, but such estimates are difficult to confirm. Roughly one-third of today's immigrants come from Africa, predominantly Senegal, Morocco, Tunisia, and Egypt. Also significant, though, is the high number of men and women from Albania, Romania, the Ukraine, Bolivia, Cape Verde, Eritrea, Ethiopia, Ghana, Iran, China, the Philippines, Sri Lanka, the United States, and countries of the former Soviet Union.[28] Women make up a large portion of these new immigrants, and domestic labor remains one of the most common forms of employment open to these women.[29] The difficulties migrants face, although similar in some ways to, say, the problems faced by Sicilians who migrated north or by southern Italians who left for North America, remain extremely different because of more pronounced linguistic, cultural, national, and racial differences between native Italians and their new neighbors.

Nonetheless, it seems only appropriate, given Italy's long-standing relationship with migration, to approach the situation with Italy's own history in mind. Such a strategy has indeed already been suggested by others. In "L'Emigrazione al femminile" Giuliana Castellani argued that:

> Io quello che sento è che questo problema degli emigrati italiani all'estero e quello degli immigrati stranieri in Italia sono due facce della stessa medaglia, dello stesso problema. E l'esperienza dell'emigrazione italiana dovrebbe servire; invece sembra che non sia servito a molto, per lottare contro il razzismo. (109)

> What I sense is that this problem of Italian emigrants abroad and of foreign immigrants in Italy are two sides of the same coin, of the same problem. The Italian emigration experience should help; instead it seems that it hasn't helped much in the battle against racism.

Castellani's "sense" has been theorized and critiqued by Verdicchio, who maintains that we can better understand Italian and Italian diasporic cultural productions if we take into consideration what migration has signified and continues to signify for people who live in Italy and for ethnic Italians elsewhere. For instance, in *Bound by Distance,* Verdicchio uses Gramsci's *The Southern Question* as a strategic point of entry into a consideration of cultural productions by recent immigrants in Italy and the political activism related to Italian autonomous social centers; he explains:

> Today it's therefore most important to analyze how the new problem of immigration is inextricably bound to the old one of emigration. A lack of appreciation for the causes and effects of the latter have often resulted in the insensitivities and ignorance that color reactions to immigrant populations.... With their own immigrant population, Italians are in many ways forced to deal with a portion of their own hidden history. (153)

Both Castellani and Verdicchio note the lack of understanding surrounding Italy's own history of migration.[30] In particular, Verdicchio reassesses Italian national history in such a way as to recognize the subaltern culture of emigrants (a theoretical move that, he argues, has not been fully "tackled by cultural critics") (169). He then places the history of emigration in dialogue with that of the contemporary story of immigration to Italy, with the hope of establishing for Italy and Italian migrants everywhere "a more coherent set of cultural alternatives" (than ones that ignore these histories) and a more "representative democracy" (169, 153). Similarly, Teresa Picarazzi, in a consideration of oral narratives by immigrant women in Italy, explains that these stories should be seen within the "context of the countless voyages that migrating women in Italian history have undergone for similar reasons, women whose stories remain buried and not relegated to the collective memory" (306). The effects of placing the different types of migration associated with Italy in a dialogic relationship—while ultimately impossible to isolate and describe—is what I examine further in these pages.

Working toward a Theory of Migration

In *Nomadic Subjects*, Rosi Braidotti outlines a feminist theory of nomadism, from which we can begin to develop a theory of migration. She emphasizes the need for a feminist theory that recognizes the "multiplicity of variables of definition of female subjectivity: race, class, age, sexual preference, and lifestyles..." (156).[31] Although nomadism, for Braidotti, can also be defined through physical movement, she stresses its association to a kind of intellectual hybridization influenced by the effects of our growing global community: "Though the image of 'nomadic subjects' is inspired by the experience of peoples or cultures that are literally nomadic, the nomadism in question here refers to the kind of critical consciousness that resists settling into socially coded modes of thought and behavior" (5). She contrasts this liberating, intellectual notion of migration with real migrant women, who leave their countries out of economic or political necessity and who "tend to be forgotten in all debates about international perspectives" (225). In her moments of extreme self-awareness, Braidotti reminds her (implicitly "First World") readers that "[i]n dealing with the becoming-subjects of women, the starting point is the politics of location, which implies the critique of dominant identities and power-formations and a sense of accountability for the historical conditions in which we share" (168). In short, she hopes to find similarities between all women while simultaneously marking their political, social, and economic differences.

Braidotti's postmodern theory of nomadism insists, troubling enough, on a distinction between the intellectual nomad and the economically driven migrant. If, instead, we focus on migration as always-already economically, intellectually, politically, and personally based, then perhaps we can avoid such pitfalls. Braidotti reminds us of the need to focus on location in discussing the movement of people; however, we might complicate her theory further by noting that immigration forces us to consider "dislocation" as central within a consideration of culture, women, and migration.

A complex notion of migration can perhaps act as an umbrella under which we shade all categories of identification and which can allow differences to function in our analyses without occlusion. Migration makes issues such as class, race, and ethnicity visible, and it also makes visible the ways the dominant culture of a nation differentiates and sometimes racializes migrants (something we will see in different ways in the representations of foreign-born domestic workers in Italy and of Italian American housewives). In other words, with an understanding of migration that takes into account various categories of identification and the power relation between and among them, we may be better able to negotiate the diverse and sometimes contradictory positions of laboring women.

It seems appropriate, then, to end this introduction with an anecdote from the 1996 Miss Italia pageant, which highlights many of the points suggested thus far and which anticipates some of the issues raised in the rest of this study. The pageant, celebrating its golden anniversary in 1996, has long been a sign of dominant Italian national and cultural identity and a surefire way of gaining public exposure for young women who wished to enter the entertainment world. Several women who went on to become international stars, Sophia Loren, Silvana Mangano, and Gina Lollobrigida, for example, were first discovered when they participated in Miss Italia. The pageant is a three-day live televised event. In 1996 the Miss Italia contest provoked widespread publicity because for the first time there was a contestant who was a woman of color, Denny Mendez, a native of the Dominican Republic, who had been living in Italy with her mother and Italian stepfather for four years. During the first night of the pageant, on live television, one of the judges, Bob Krieger, an Egyptian-born, Jewish Italian photojournalist, made a telling remark about the slim chances of a black contestant winning the crown, a remark which implied, however indirectly, that there was a certain representative "look" connected to being Italian that a woman of color could never achieve.[32] His comment caused an immediate outcry, and the following day the *padrone* of the pageant, Enzo Mirigliani, dismissed Krieger from the jury. Two days later Denny Mendez was crowned Miss Italia, by both in-studio judges and public televotes (by an overwhelming majority). In dismissing Krieger, Mirigliani noted among other things the routine mistreatment of southern Italians by northerners throughout Italian history, recalling in particular his own father's difficulty finding a place to live and work when he emigrated to northern Italy. He linked Italy's past history of emigration and internal migration to the country's current status as a home to new immigrants and suggested that Mendez's participation in his contest could be used as a national example against anti-immigrant sentiment.

Mendez's win marked the end of a charade at least fifty years old that assumed that the Italian woman has an identifiable "look," a set of physical and racial characteristics that set her apart from, say, a French woman, a Japanese woman, or an American woman. Interestingly, at least one other contestant was not born in Italy, Maria Mazza, New Jersey-born of Neapolitan parents, the second runner-up. Needless to say, the ethnic identity of this Sophia Loren look-alike did not come up in journalists' pageant postmortems. The intense public debate around race that Mendez's participation in the pageant provoked (a debate that was visible in the media and on the streets) points to the tension provoked by migration. The fact that this public debate on race arose from a beauty pageant says something, perhaps, about the degree to which rigid gender roles are bound up in the imagined community of the Italian state—that is, while the media claimed public outrage or at least confusion over the idea that Mendez could represent Italy, there were no such reports of public concerns about the sexist nature of beauty contests.

The fact that Mirigliani brought up Italy's own history of migration in order to foreground the discrimination Mendez first received versus the immediate acceptance Mazza received can be helpful in thinking about women workers, both as real historical beings and as characters represented via a variety of cultural texts. For instance, we can imagine that the extremely different reaction these two women received to some extent parallels the experiences of Italian-born domestics and foreign-born domestics, since one of the main forms of employment open to women of color in Italy today is domestic work.[33] Mary Romero, in her groundbreaking study *Maid in the U.S.A.*, considers the experiences of Chicanas within the domestic work sphere and traces the history of domestic labor in the United States, focusing on issues of class and race. Romero explains how in the past, domestic service in the United States created a means for immigrants to assimilate to mainstream, middle-class America: "The occupation has long been described as an entry-level position for immigrants which offers social mobility to foreign-born women and their children to move on to higher-status and better-paying jobs" (27). As such, the labor helped create and sustain a middle-class cultural/national identity that upheld traditional, patriarchal beliefs and norms. Continuing, she explains that reformers "praised the work" because it "was not only a sure way of modernizing traditional, rural, ethnic women but also offered the means for social mobility" (27). Yet for women of color such mobility usually is thwarted in part by the way they are treated by their employers, and the occupation is more like an "occupational ghetto"—thus assimilation to middle-class culture remains less of a possibility for women of color (27). Accordingly, Mendez's participation in the Miss Italia pageant—traditionally a step toward employment in entertainment for Italian women—threatens the stability of unwritten rules sustaining domestic labor and other such unskilled work as the only avenue for immigrant women of color in Italy. Mendez sidestepped traditional types of employment open to women of color in Italy (like domestic labor) and opted instead to participate in an event that would more likely offer her social mobility.

Furthermore, Mendez's participation and victory in the Miss Italia pageant effectively disrupts dominant notions about Italian national identity. The comparison between Mendez and Mazza shows how cultural identity can almost determine national identity. While both Mendez and Mazza were naturalized citizens, Mazza's cultural connection (and "racial") to the peninsula gave her the right to represent it, whereas Mendez's lack of such a connection, coupled by her racialized migrant status, made her a threatening presence in the contest. The emergence of Denny Mendez in Italy marks one of the effects of the country's history of migration, and it points to the necessity of a consideration of labor and migrant women in a broad Italian context.

This Book

The critical readings in the following chapters rely on a theoretical feminist foundation built upon a consideration of Antonio Gramsci's reconfiguration of Marxist categories and a nuanced understanding of migration. Gramsci's ideas on the development of national popular culture that counters the dominant culture especially in relation to his emphasis on everyday practices and "folklore," his unique understanding of language and "common sense," his call for alliances across different subaltern classes, and his emphasis on organic intellectuals all fundamentally inform my close readings. None of these ideas are distinct and each relies to different degrees on one another.

The following chapters focus on four different types of labor, all within an Italian context, broadly defined: Chapter one considers cultural productions that chronicle the lives of Italian female rice workers, or *mondine*; chapter two looks at the changing identity (as shown through different narratives) of female domestic servants in Italy in the second half of the twentieth century; chapter three considers cinematic representations of unwaged household work among Italian American women; and chapter four offers an overview of female immigrant cannery labor in California in relation to photographic histories. A suggestive epilogue on the writing of photographer Tina Modotti closes the book. The categories of labor sectors discussed herein are by no means exhaustive and are only meant to be a sampling of the different ways in which migrant women workers take part in the development of the complexities of national popular culture, even as they are excluded from dominant formations of culture.

Notes

1. "Lavorare è anche il mio modo di essere donna, di amare, di partecipare alla vita, capisci?" The screenplay for *Le amiche* was written by Suso Cecchi D'Amico, Alba de Cespedes, and Antonioni. All translations, unless otherwise noted, are mine.

2. By "Italian" I mean both the country "Italy" and people or culture defined as "Italian." I define migrant within an Italian context to mean a person who moves seasonally or permanently to or from Italy or who moves internally within Italy.

3. As Michael Hardt and Antonio Negri remind us in their co-authored *Empire*, by the end of World War II Italy was "predominantly peasant-based" and reached an industrialized state late, in comparison to most of its European neighbors, and therefore has a different narrative of development, one that places it historically somewhat outside of the borders of the so-called First World (289).

4. In relation to Italy, see, for example, Giorgio Candelora's "Lo sviluppo del capitalismo e del movimento operario" in his *Storia dell'Italia moderna* (Vol. VI). Candelora discusses the birth of Socialism in Italy and the worker's movements with barely a nod to agricultural or other kinds of labor and with little discussion of the relationship between migration and the worker's movement. Candeolora brings up agricultural labor mainly in his study of Fascism. See also Di Scala, who discusses agricultural movements, but only in relation to how they affect the industrialization of

Italy: "Economic historians agree that important gains in agricultural production per unit precede or accompany rapid industrial expansion and continued growth" (146). For an example of an historical study which *does* consider in detail the significance of agricultural movements, see John A. Davis's *Gramsci and Italy's Passive Revolution*. In Davis's collection there are two brief references to the existence of rice production in Italy (115 and 172). In U.S. histories most of the historical and/or ethnographic studies on Italian American women have to do with factory and sweatshop work especially in and around New York City and do not spend much time on other kinds of labor. See, for instance, Louise C. Odencrantz's *Italian Women in Industry* or Nancy Green's *Ready-to-Wear and Ready-to-Work*. A more complex look at Italian American women and labor is Miriam Cohen's *Workshop to Office*, which sketches Italian American women's move from the working class to the middle class over two generations. Another interesting text is the now-classic testimonial, *Rosa, the Life of an Italian Immigrant*. This turn-of-the-century autobiography of an Italian immigrant woman living in Chicago was transcribed by Marie Hall Ets, a social worker.

5. Most information about working women, including factory workers, is to be found in feminist histories. In relation to Italy see, for instance, the work of Franca Pieroni Bortolotti and of the Italian feminist groups, *Diotima* and *Rivolta femminile*. See also the work of Donna Gabaccia, such as, *Women, Gender, and Transnational Lives: Italian Workers of the World* (edited with Franca Iacovetta). See also Martin Clark, who notes the lack of information about Italian women, especially concerning the nineteenth century. Much has been written in the last twenty-five years about Italian and Italian American women's role as "Rosie the Riveter" during the World War II. On this phenomenon, see, for example, Mafai, De Grazia and Birnbaum. For a history of women's experiences in Great Britain during both world wars see Braybon and Summerfield; for U.S. women during World War II see Gluck. For scholarship about Italian American working women, see footnote four.

6. Mohanty is critical, in particular, of ethnographic work she sees being done by Western feminists about so-called Third World women: "I would like to suggest that the feminist writings I analyze here discursively colonize the material and historical heterogenities of the lives of women in the third world, thereby producing/ re-presenting a composite, singular 'third world woman'—an image which appears arbitrarily constructed, but nevertheless carries with it the authorizing signature of Western humanist discourse" (53). For a useful review of the kind of feminist historiography I am aligning myself with see Lisa Lowe and David Lloyd's introduction to their edited collection, *The Politics of Culture in the Shadow of Capital*; see, in particular, pages 16–27 for a discussion of feminism as it relates to the production and dissemination of culture on to the transnational terrain.

7. She defines "Americanization" not only as changing nationality but also "the initiation of people into an emerging industrial and consumer society . . . [which] had an impact that went beyond the immigrants themselves and touched the lives of most of the people who might be called Americans, transforming the way of life of a large proportion of the population" (15).

8. See, for instance, *Are Italians White?* (eds. Jennifer Guglielmo and Salvatore Salerno) discussed in later chapters. See also Lisa Lowe's *Immigrant Acts*, in particular chapters one, five, and seven for an analysis of the sometimes conflicting determinations of race, class, and gender with respect to a discussion of Asian American culture, transnationalism, labor, and history.

9. Roediger's study on the ways in which the white working class began using their whiteness as a "wage" (a term borrowed from W. E. B. Du Bois) will have more immediate relevance to my considerations of Italian American women. In his introduction he outlines the lack of scholarship that combines race and class. He explains that "general histories of racism . . . rely mainly on evidence from political leaders, intellectuals and scientists"; that studies of "race and popular culture generally do not explore the difficult question of the specific roles of the working class in creating popular culture treatments of race nor the specific meanings of racism in popular culture for workers"; and that research that does combine race and work "mainly stay on the terrain of trade union practices regarding race" (10). Suffice it to say that when discussing the white working class' acceptance of racism, studies rely on "overly simple economic explanations" (10).

10. See Zappi, in particular pages 238–242. She explains that the women deserted the rice fields, set up "propaganda committees," held rallies, and led marches (238). Later she concludes that "[The women rice workers'] cooperation in organizing the June 1914 general strike (Red Week) . . . is a sign of their interest in playing a larger role in public life, and of their concern about issues transcending the limits of the rice belt . . ." (276).

11. We should recall that Gramsci's letters are in no way ordinary personal correspondence, since they were conceived in prison and were under strict Fascist censors. Gramsci himself commented occasionally on this odd form of writing, sometimes stating what might seem like a common feeling in our day of spontaneous electronic messages: To Julia, he writes, "Se dovessi io stesso rileggere le mie lettere dopo qualche settimana, mi pare che ne proverei un certo disgusto" ("If I were to reread my letters after a few weeks I think I would find them a bit distasteful") (*Lettere* 186). Other times he called specific attention to his lack of privacy, again to his wife: "Le mie lettere sono 'pubbliche,' non riservate a noi due" ("My letters are 'public,' not reserved for us two") (*Lettere* 188).

12. Gramsci explains that "Domostroi" is an anonymous Russian text from the sixteenth century which called for a conservative familial household (142).

13. Although it is difficult to say with any sense of exactness when Gramsci wrote the different sections of what is now collected in his *Notebooks*, the "Americanism and Fordism" sections seems to have been first composed in 1934, three years after the letters quoted herein (see David Forgacs's notes in Gramsci's *Reader*, 15).

14. Gramsci uses the example of prohibition in the United States as a "tendency" which was dealt with privately and then became "state ideology" (*Reader* 291). Much of his study of U.S. business practices was related to his interest in Ital-

ian Fascism. He was not wrong to see that private matters (such as sexuality) could one day be regulated by the state in order to raise capital—in fact, Mussolini, in his effort to build his army and his empire, entered the bedrooms of Italians, outlawing homosexuality, taxing bachelors, and offering insubstantial gifts to women who had many children.

15. While Gramsci's use of the term *hegemony* changes in different texts, we can say that it refers most consistently to the relationship between classes and the strategy by which a ruling class maintains consent (not through force), and by which a revolutionary strategy (often referred to by Gramsci scholars as a counter-hegemony) depends on the formation of alliances across different groups in order to overthrow the ruling class's hegemony.

16. Such an insistence on power relations and the structure of consent and rebellion within civil society brings to mind the work of Michel Foucault, and Holub turns to Foucault for filling in the holes left by Gramsci's own theory of sexuality: "What Gramsci and Foucault share . . . is the notion that power and domination function in so far as those dominated consent to that domination" (199).

17. Landy uses the term "subaltern" very loosely to refer to any disenfranchised person or group. While I am wary of such an overarching definition, I think in this case "woman" can be replaced with "subaltern."

18. Gramsci distinguishes only slightly between "folklore" and "common sense," calling "folklore" a "conception of the world and life implicit to a large extent in determinate . . . strata of society and in opposition to . . . 'official' conceptions of the world," and he calls "common sense" a "philosophical folklore" (*Reader* 360).

19. In Gramsci's notes see "The Formation of the Intellectual" ("La formazine degli intellettuali" in *Gli intellettuali e l'organizzazione della cultura*).

20. As Sasson explains, Gramsci's class-based nationalism depends on the formation of a "war of position" whereby all forms of culture produced by the people are recognized for their inherent political power: "The historical task of the proletariat is to create a society in which politics in its narrow sense decreases and in which politics in its widest sense, including civil society or 'self-government' becomes the norm" (Sasson 130). For Gramsci, war of position is usually associated with a hegemony created by the left. As David Forgacs points out, Gramsci also used the term "war of position" to explain "a phase of 'revolution-reaction' or passive revolution," such as Fascism, "which modernizes the economy 'from above' by breaking the political power of both the laissez-faire bourgeoisie and the organized working class" (*Gramsci's Reader*, 428–429). (A "war of position" is opposed to a "war of maneuver," a more revolutionary approach to cultural and political change.) In Stuart Hall's "Gramsci's Relevance for the Study of Race and Ethnicity," Hall explains "war of position" in his own words: It "has to be conducted in a protracted way, across many different and varying fronts of struggle; where there is rarely a single break-through which wins the war once and for all" (Hall 37).

21. See my coauthored introduction to *Italian Neorealism and Global Cinema* for a similar discussion of national popular culture, this time in relation to cinema.

22. Gramsci uses the two words "national popular" (*nazionale popolare*) because he wants a phrase that means both "from the people" and "from the nation" and finds no such term in Italian. He explains:

> In Italia il termine "nazionale" ha un significato molto ristretto ideologicamente e in ogni caso non coincide con "popolare," perché in Italia gli intellettuali sono lontani dal popolo, cioè dalla "nazione" e sono invece legati a una tradizione di casta, che non è mai stata rotta da un forte movimento politico popolare o nazionale dal basso. (Letteratura 123)

> In Italy the term "national" has an ideologically very restricted meaning, and does not in any case coincide with "popular" because in Italy the intellectuals are distant from the people, i.e., from the "nation." They are tied to a caste tradition that has never been broken by strong popular or national popular movements from below. (Gramsci, *Reader* 366)

23. Bakhtin and Gramsci have been discussed together by others as well. In comparing the two, Michael Gardiner notes, among other things, that Bakhtin viewed civil systems and dominant culture as "monologic," while Gramsci thought cultural hegemony by subaltern groups was possible exactly because the civil systems and dominant culture were "dialogic" (*pace* Bakhtin). Gramsci felt that "no matter how successful hegemony was at securing the 'historical bloc,' he believed that the maintenance of consent necessitated a certain amount of freedom with respect to the internal elaboration of popular forms of thought and culture. . . . He also asserted that regional dialects, local customs, songs, proverbs . . . represented a force which contested the absolute domination of a hegemonic culture and ideology" (Gardiner 184). For another comparison of the two thinkers see David Shepherd in Hirschkop and Shephard.

24. Bakhtin defines "speech genres" as follows: "Each separate utterance is individual, of course, but each sphere in which language is used develops its own *relatively stable types* of these utterances. These we may call *speech genres*" (emphasis in original, *Speech Genres* 60).

25. The "author debate" remains unsettled among Bakhtin scholars, some of whom argue that Voloshinov, Medevev, and Bakhtin were in fact the same person; others believe the three may have collaborated in different ways on certain texts. One of the more contested aspects of the debate is the obvious Marxist perspective of Voloshinov's work and the often less-outwardly Marxist perspective of Bakhtin's work. The facts suggest that, at the very least, Bakhtin and Voloshinov shared ideas with each other and moved within similar circles. See the chapter "The Disputed Texts," in Morson and Emerson or Hirschkop and Shepherd (196–197).

26. See Absalom, Candelora, Clark, and Di Scala for a more detailed history of migration and Italy. Precise numbers of migrants are difficult to attain because of the presumed high number of emigrants who returned home each year, some who would later migrate to another city or country. Nevertheless we can piece together the following statistics. For the sake of consistency, here all numbers are those found in

Martin Clark's *Modern Italy*; however, his numbers are in line with those of other historians. Italian emigration to European countries was at about 100,000 a year in the 1890s. In particular the Veneto region "provided practically half the European migrants by 1886–1888, and nearly two-thirds ten years later" (Clark 33). Most of the southern emigration to the Americas occurred between 1898 and 1914, with at least 150,000 Italians crossing each year (165). The decline in emigration to the Americas and Europe seems to have been caused by a number of reasons, including changes in U.S. admittance policies (they "had taken 233,000 Italian immigrants a year on average between 1901 and 1910 . . . in the 1920s they took 42,000, and in the 1930s 11,500"), World War I, the Depression, and Mussolini's regulations on leaving the country and on persuading recent emigrants to return (273). These factors caused a shift in emigration that resulted in increased internal migration—more and more people moving from rural areas to urban areas beginning in the 1920s (273).

27. For a sense of the magnitude of this "postwar migration," we can look at the southern regions, where most emigrants came from; between 1951 and 1971 over 3 million southerners left their hometowns (Clark 360).

28. It seems relevant to note the high number of documented U.S. citizens residing in Italy. Looking back, we find that by October 1998 there were approximately 44,600 U.S. citizens who claimed residency in Italy, a higher number than, for instance, documented Tunisians (41,000). The U.S. citizens (a mix of professionals and returning emigrants, the latter being a relatively new phenomenon) are not usually mentioned in discussions of extracomunitari even though they do fit the definition. The term *extracomunitari*, usually used negatively by the media, has become a euphemism for "people of color." Americans, because they are not considered immigrants, become detached from the term extracomunitari, which results in a faulty assumption that all Americans are white and that no American could be undocumented. Ignoring U.S. immigration to Italy continues to reaffirm a binary between the "West" and "non-West" and aggravates the racist assumption that immigration is threatening and burdensome to the "receiving" nation. Moreover, it adds a noteworthy twist to the current academic discussions of Italian Americans and whiteness. See Jennifer Guglielmo and Salvatore Salerno's *Are Italians White?*

29. The actual numbers and nations of origin of Italian immigrants is difficult to know because of bureaucratic immigration laws and the high number of undocumented workers. In his *States of Grace*, Donald Martin Clark notes the impossibility of quantifying immigration to Italy:

> The categories of numbers, regions, and economic variables could not chart the far reaches of a population hidden in the world of work. . . . Beyond the marginal estimates of the migrants' numbers on the tables of the minister of labor, transnational migrants are only visible in the sensational tracks in the papers, and in the investigative reporting of the newscasts that place "blacks" just where commonsense dictates. (126)

30. For a similar consideration of the relationship between emigration from Italy and immigration to Italy (one which relies on a Gramscian reading as well), see Donald Martin Clark's *States of Grace*. See chapters seven and eight in particular.

31. Irene Gedaf's critique ("Can Nomads Learn to Count to Four? Rosi Braidotti and the Space for Difference in Feminist Theory") of Braidotti's book superbly outlines the elitist trappings of Braidotti's feminist model. See also Caren Kaplan's "The Politics of Location as Transnational Feminist Critical Practice," for a useful intervention on the subject of postcolonialism, postmodernism, and feminist practice.

32. One of Krieger's most dubious remarks was that "a black woman can't win a competition that's meant to reward and represent Italian beauty" (in Gennari 72). In an interview with *L'Unità* writer Marcella Ciarnelli, Mendez said: "Mi sento profondamente italiana . . ." ("I feel profoundly Italian . . .") (14). Meanwhile, two days later, Krieger told Ciarnelli that "non basta avere il passaporto italiano per esserlo [rappresentante dell'Italia]" ("an Italian passport is not enough [to represent Italy]") (9).

33. Although paid domestic work will be taken up in chapter two, it is helpful at this point to know that until the 1970s, paid domestic work in Italy was mainly the domain of working-class Italian women; now it is mainly performed by immigrant women of color.

CHAPTER ONE

Italian Rice Workers and National Popular Culture

Se non ci conoscete
guardateci negli occhi
noi siamo le compagne della Maria Margotti

—Traditional rice worker song[1]

Forgotten except for a brief mention in a 1984 history book on the Italian rice workers, the above-quoted song memorializes a heroine and martyr of agricultural workers. Maria Margotti, as much neglected as the song that tells her story, was a rice worker (*mondina*) killed by an Italian military policeman (*carabiniere*) during an agricultural strike in Molinella on May 17, 1949.[2] The strike in which she was participating was part of a national labor action (including workers from both the north and the south) which ended, after thirty-seven days, with the signing of the first national contract for agricultural workers.[3] Margotti's death made the front pages of the leftist newspapers in Italy, and she was eulogized by, among others, the Cgil-funded supplement, *Per te mondina*:

> 17 maggio 1949: già da qualche giorno tutti i braccianti Italiani sono in sciopero contro la miseria, contro lo sfruttamento degli agrari. Le mondine della Valle Padana sono in prima fila, gli agrari tentano di arginarne la forza organizzando il crumiraggio. Le mondine si avvicinano ai crumiri, parlano loro e li convincono a tornare alle loro case di montagna.

> A Molinella, su di un argine vicino alla strada sono cinque donne: passa una motocicletta, una voce ordina alle donne di andarsene. Poi si ode uno sparo, una delle donne cade. Muore Maria Margotti, una donna di 34 anni, vedova già da sei anni che con il suo lavoro estenuante di mondina ha allevato le sue due bambine. Muore eroicamente una donna che insieme alle sue compagne cercava solo di difendere il suo diritto al lavoro, il diritto di dare del pane alle sue figlie.
>
> Nel suo nome, oggi, tutte le mondine d'Italia continuano le loro lotte per la difesa di quei diritti per i quali Maria Margotti ha sacrificato la sua giovane vita.[4]

In death Margotti became a martyr and heroine for the rice workers, as well as a symbol of their struggles and exploitation. While the feminist movements of the seventies sparked a renewed interest in the rice workers, Margotti remains a relatively obscure figure in the annals of Italian history.

This chapter explores possible answers to this question: Why have the *mondine*, a group of women agricultural workers, been significantly neglected in Italian history, even though, since the 1600s, their work has been a vital part of the culture and livelihood of what is now the northern regions of Italy? In intervening on this question I propose the *mondine* can, by means of synecdoche, stand for other exploited groups in Italy; further, their history and the representation of that history can be read in such a way as to force us to question and contest various aspects of the past and the way we view that past. Critiquing various cultural representations of the rice workers has the potential to shift long-standing notions about Italian history in relation to the creation of national popular culture. The creative cultural productions that focus on rice labor, and the authors of these cultural texts, have summarily been overlooked by critics and historians or have been criticized for their efforts to represent the rice workers. Therefore, an important component of this historiographic project is to recuperate certain cultural pieces that deal with rice workers and that challenge us to think about migratory labor as integral to national identity. As such, here I offer a brief history of rice labor, in part to account for some of the reasons for their critical neglect. From this historical reconstruction I move to a discussion of creative representations of the workers, focusing on two different artistic mediums: their own tradition of singing and the writing of Renata Viganò. The contemporary musical group *Coro delle mondine* acts as an example of a counter-hegemonic national popular culture, produced by a subaltern class. Meanwhile Viganò's work reminds us of the need for alliances in order to overturn the hegemony that helps support and is supported by the nation-state. These interventions suggest ways in which the representations of migratory female labor are implicated in the culture of the nation-state at the same time as they may counter or offer alternatives to that power structure.

The *Mondine*: A History Lesson

Historically, the Italian rice belt—mainly the Po Valley in Lombardia and parts of Emilia-Romagna—offered employment opportunities for both men and women, but since at least the seventeenth century, labor has been divided along gender lines, with women taking the jobs of weeders and planters. The first records of group rice worker protests are from the mid-nineteenth century, and by later in that century, the antagonism between the landowners and the *mondine* took the shape of small organized group protests and strikes. The formation of the Italian Socialist Party (PSI) in 1891, backed mainly by men, further aided in this surge, because it immediately began to organize the women rice weeders. This brief history of the *mondine* is not written in standard Italian history books or in Italian labor histories.[5] Indeed, this history is only found in feminist-influenced revisionist histories or in government documents, newspapers, and creative texts. The three history books devoted solely to the history of rice workers, published in the 1980s and early 1990s, rely heavily on official government documents, ephemera, and oral accounts.[6] As Zappi explains at the beginning of the bibliography to *If Eight Hours Seem too Few*:

> It is necessary to emphasize the importance that socialist and labor newspapers have in this attempt at exploring the weeders' history. Without their existence, this research would have been almost impossible. Although there are alternate sources, there are some gaps in the unpublished materials held in the rice-belt archives and in the *Archivio Centrale dello Stato* in Rome. . . . The lacunas in these archival holdings . . . limit the researcher's access to the official version of the events through which the weeders became a visible group on the national scene. (357)

In the introduction to another historical text about the women workers, *Quando saremo a Reggio Emilia* (edited by Marco Paterlini), there lies a possible answer as to why their situation is so often disregarded—Otello Montanari and Gianfranco Riccò explain the uniqueness of the *mondine*'s labor: "Sono lavoratrici precarie, sradicate dal proprio ambiente per raggiungere le zone di lavoro, sono donne che lasciano i tradizionali compiti domestici per trasformarsi in 'operaie-massa'" ("They are precarious workers, uprooted from their environment in order to reach work areas, they are women who leave behind their traditional domestic chores and transform themselves into 'mass workers'") (in Paterlini 7). In other words, the rice workers do not conform to standard notions about the composition of labor groups. As seasonal migrant women working outside of the home, they are by definition an unusual group; this unusualness could explain in part why they are not present in chronicles about Italy's past. Most of the women who worked in the rice fields came from villages from the northern regions of Emilia-Romagna, Lombardia, Piemonte, and the Veneto and had to migrate temporarily for the forty-day weeding season. The women also differed by age, marital status, and to a lesser extent, level of education. Some left their families behind and traveled alone, others came with sisters or cousins, and on occasion the women brought along their young children.

Traditionally, church policies and social constraints limited women's involvement in labor protests. Even the PSI, presumably a space where longstanding traditions were broken, only organized a few women's leagues (*leghe femminili*); moreover, women weeders were rarely present at these meetings.[7] Instead, the men tended to dominate these groups—they planned, ran, and attended the meetings. On the women's constraints to organize, Zappi writes:

> The men—husbands, brothers, fathers—were delegates for the women of the family. Time-honored tradition confined women to the home; men took care of public affairs. The church was one deterrent to weeders' forming their own leagues. However, strong male opposition hindered them as well. They were living under the two-fold pressure of wage work and housework, and under the stern eye of a husband, brother, or father who would disapprove of any activity beyond supplementing the family income and taking care of the home and children. (108)

The Socialists made some effort to involve more women, though. For instance, in a 1906 strike at Vercelli they publicly called for women to take the place of male relatives who had emigrated. In effect, the PSI tapped into a useful resource. Women free from male authority and support were again and again compelled to be more independent and resourceful within public life.[8] What is clear, though, is that women rice workers who wanted to participate openly in protest movements had to deal with male authority as well as the Catholic Church's authority, both of which permeated their entire lives.

Yet some women ignored cultural limitations or found creative ways around them, even when male authority was close to home and the church was in sight. For instance, during the 1906 strikes, many women broke conventional gender roles by borrowing certain aspects of an accepted role expendable in their protests. In an odd mix of Socialist politics and Catholic traditions, the "weeders, accompanied by other women sympathizers and children, donned clothes they kept for festivals and marched solemnly, as though they were parading in a religious procession. This was a ritual they were much more familiar with" (Zappi 264). Even the everyday life of the *mondine* can be understood as a "break from family oppression, from their daily routine, and from the heavy control of the traditional milieu" (Zappi 23). To see weeding as liberating risks ignoring obvious and powerful forces which brought and kept women returning year after year to the rice fields. Nonetheless, we can imagine the benefits of being surrounded by the support and friendship of other women, especially since many women were away from home and facing a back-breaking labor. Thus we can understand some of the reasons why their status as a category of workers is precarious, unconventional, and consequently often overlooked.

We can perhaps best understand some of the effects of the abandonment of conventional roles if we consider briefly the outcome of the 1906 Vercelli strike, where the rice workers were asking for a restricted eight-hour work day. Zappi explains that this strike was the largest up to that date; it grew swiftly across the area and was in fact comprised of a number of smaller strikes and protest actions.[9] The long-term meaningful consequences of the strike lie in the unprecedented solidarity of workers rather than in its effectiveness in improving labor conditions—though there were major changes in the farm labor field. The initial *mondine* strikers persuaded all the workers in the areas to protest. The solidarity among workers crossed gender lines, with men and women protesting together. Interestingly, the actions of the *mondine* repeatedly instigated this united struggle for labor bargaining, even though women had usually neither been expected nor asked to participate in such political actions. Considering the traditional gender roles the workers were encouraged to sustain, their ability to achieve unity at the 1906 strike is particularly exceptional.

A student of Italian history and culture does indeed have a difficult time tracking the *mondine*, not only because of the temporary nature of their employment, but also because of the women's abandonment of traditional activities, and the diversity among the women themselves. On the other hand, we can turn their seemingly unusualness around and view it as a characteristic that better lends itself to critical consideration. For example, their differences (in age, marital status, or dialect, for instance) is exactly what allows us to identify them as representative of all Italian female peasants, a point that Zappi, Gualandi, and Montanari and Riccò all make subtly when referring to the *mondine*'s participation in national and international movements, like labor rights actions and 1960s-era peace protests.

Most of the remaining contemporary critical acknowledgment of the women's position in Italian history has to do with their involvement in World War II. For example, Victoria De Grazia in *How Fascism Ruled Women* explains that by the time Mussolini was in power, rice was a flourishing crop that employed thousands of women yearly. She also offers us a description of the workers' lives:

> In late spring each year about two hundred thousand women, at least a quarter of whom were under twenty-one years of age, traveled by train, by truck and on foot to staging areas at Vercelli, Novara and Cremona for the eight-week rice "campaign." Starting in early May, when the misty dawns were still freezing, and finishing in July, when suffocating heat settled over the swampy fields, the women, in three reprises, waded waist-deep into the muddy paddies to sow, weed, and harvest the crops. (182)

In addition, De Grazia indirectly refers to the *mondine*'s worker movements when she explains the Fascists' attempt at regulating the *mondine*. Mussolini had high stakes in the regulation of the rice workers, because rice was to replace in part the more expensive, imported wheat in the Italian diet. He soon met with worker rebellion, however, which De Grazia argues came from the *mondine*'s relationship to the PSI: the *mondine* "had been the mainstay of rural socialism" (183). The rice workers were, in fact, the only labor group to gain from their labor actions during fascism. Between 1931 and 1934 they held numerous strikes, and "in pieno fascismo le *mondine* sono l'unica categoria di lavoratrici che sciopera, e riesce ad ottenere migliori condizioni di vita" ("at the height of Fascism, the *mondine* are the only group of workers who strike and manage to obtain better living conditions") (*Per te mondina*). The fact that a peasant group, especially a predominantly female peasant group, could successfully protest Fascism is a reality ignored again and again in many histories of the *Ventennio*, the twenty years of Fascist rule. The women are given credit for their actions, however, in revisionist histories, including Gualandi's, in which she quotes the political activist and author, Teresa Noce, describing the events (32–33); Lucia Chiavola Birnbaum's *liberazione delle donne*, in which she mentions in passing the rice worker strikes under Fascism (29); and by Luigi Arbizzani in the journal of the *Istituto Alcide Cervi*, in which he discusses workers' involvement in the World War II Resistance in the Valle Padana and pays particular attention to the contribution of the *mondine*.[10]

Self-Representation

Other aspects of the lives and struggles of the *mondine* have been depicted in a variety of creative texts, most of which have been all but forgotten by scholars. A brief survey of these texts gives us, in chronological order: Marchesa Colombi's 1878 novel *In risaia* (*In the Rice Field*),[11] which uses Zola-style naturalism and romanticized popular fiction conventions to illustrate the horrible conditions of the *mondine*; some of Ada Negri's 1892 poems in *Fatalità*,[12] which examine, in lyric form, the hardships of their work; Giuseppe De Santis's 1949 film *Riso amaro* (*Bitter Rice*), which details the difficult labor of the *mondine* and the sexual politics at play in the rice fields; Renata Viganò's 1952 *Le mondine* (*The Women Rice Workers*), a collection of essays that were previously published on the pages of *L'Unità*; Davide Lajolo's 1955 novel *Quaranta giorni, quaranta notti* (*Forty Days, Forty Nights*), which follows a woman during her first experience as a rice worker and her first encounters with labor protests in a didactic and suspenseful narrative that originally appeared in *Noi donne* in serialized form in 1952; Fausta Cialente's short story, "Viaggio in risaia" ("Voyage in the Rice Fields"), which depicts the duress of the rice fields and was published in *Noi donne* in 1953; and, lastly, the *mondine* have been the subject of countless paintings and photographs throughout the years.[13] None of the aforementioned creative or critical pieces were produced by a former *mondina*, perhaps a sign of the lack of opportunity open to the women.[14] In order to hear their own voices, then, we must turn to the songs they created. Such self-representation is at the core of Gramsci's notion of national popular culture—a positioning of one's cultural identity that is at some level self-conscious and directed.

During work and strike actions *mondine* often took to singing. Their repertoire included songs describing the burden of their work, social customs, and past protest experiences—thus singing is both a form of resistance and a kind of living oral history, creating a kind of Gramscian national popular culture born of folk culture: "Il canto è nello stesso tempo, incitamento ritmico al lavoro, dichiarazione di lotta e sollievo, ma è anche dimostrazione concreta della spesso ignorata capacità delle donne della campagna di produrre cultura" ("Song is at once an encouraging rhythm to work, a declaration of struggle and relief, but it is also a concrete demonstration of country women's often-ignored capacity to produce culture") (in Paterlini 8). Many of their songs are as recognizable to most Italians as "I've Been Workin' on the Railroad" or "Yankee Doodle" is to anyone who attended U.S. elementary schools. In fact, the songs have entered "nella storia, nel folclore vivo" ("into history, into the current folklore") of Italy, suggesting a movement from "common sense" toward the formation of national popular culture (Gualandi 68). Their presence in twentieth-century Italian national popular culture is further strengthened through the Coro delle mondine di Correggio, a group of former *mondine* who perform and record rice worker songs.

Interestingly, in performance the Coro delle mondine link their work as *mondine* to the partisan struggle. For instance, when the *Coro delle mondine* closed Bologna Sogna, the city's summer arts festival in 1996, history was fore-grounded in their performance. Singing to a Piazza Maggiore filled with mostly Italian twenty-somethings looking for a good time, the Coro delle mondine roused the crowd with traditional work songs. After initial ironic comments about seeing *nonna* up on stage, the young crowd joined in with what is one of the more familiar tunes of the *mondine*, "Bella ciao"—sung in medley format with another version of "Bella ciao," the World War II Resistance version. Similarly, on the Coro's album, *Mondariso*, they sing the *mondina* version of "Bella ciao" ("Alla mattina apena alzata/in risaia me tocca andar/E fra gli insetti e le zanzare/un dur lavoro mi tocca far"[15]), ending it with a verse from the partisan version ("O partigiano portami via/che mi sento di morir"[16]). Although its origins are debatable, "Bella ciao" seems to have started as a *mondina* protest song. The two versions feature the same melody and a similar refrain.[17] Regardless of the songs' past, they are now inevitably connected, as made clear by the effortless way the Coro delle mondine and the audience moved from one version to the other. Likewise, the messages within each song become equally intertwined: The rice workers' protest against their *padroni* parallels the partisans' protests against the Fascists. Historical events, such as the *mondine* strikes during Fascism, link these two issues, and the way they are kept alive in the national popular culture of Italy further strengthens this relationship.

The Story of Two Women: Maria Margotti and Renata Viganò

Setting up relationships between various past events is a common trait of the rice worker's musical verse. Some of their songs came from labor actions and thus formed an immediate kind of historical record of the events, accessible to all who can hear. From the 1906 Vercelli strike came the now-classic "Se otto ore vi sembran poche" ("If eight hours seem like few to you"), and from the 1949 strike came the song from which my epigraph comes, memorializing Margotti. Yet another historical link between Fascism and labor protests is to be found in the rice worker, Maria Margotti, who had been a partisan during World War II. Turning back to the historical figure of Margotti, we quickly realize that she remains a relatively unknown figure even in texts on Italian labor history. To learn about Margotti one must look to hard-to-find, out-of-print books and newspaper clippings. My search for information about Margotti began and always seems to come back to the writer Renata Viganò. In fact, Viganò and her husband, Antonio Meluschi, both penned newspaper pieces about Margotti at the time of her death, and as long as Viganò wrote for *Noi donne*, the paper yearly commemorated Margotti's death. Moreover, Gualandi, in her 1984 historical study of the *mondine*, relies on Viganò's work in her discussion of Margotti. By writing about Margotti's life and death, Viganò strengthened Margotti's link to other workers and at the same time discursively created a historical figure. Viganò, in many ways, wrote Margotti-as-historical-figure into existence by repeatedly referring to her and her struggles. As such, Viganò's and Margotti's lives intertwine in ways that foreground Gramsci's emphasis on the need to build alliances and subaltern representation in order to achieve political change.

Viganò is usually remembered for her award-winning Resistance novel, *L'Agnese va a morire*, a story that follows the actions of an elderly washerwoman as she is prompted to take up arms and join the armed Resistance movement of World War II.[18] Yet Viganò was a prolific writer—her works range from poetry, short stories, novels, and pieces of journalism. When we look to those dusty, rarely read pages, we find that Viganò again and again championed the rights of the underrepresented.[19] From landless farm workers to unwed mothers, Viganò continued to expose the lives of some of Italy's most exploited and forgotten people.[20] Her writing became more politically charged after the publication and success of *L'Agnese va a morire*. Her essays and poetry frequently appeared on the pages of *L'Unità*, *Noi donne*, and *Il Progresso d'Italia*, and her readership grew. By the early 1950s, the popularity she had gained from the publication of *L'Agnese va a morire* afforded her a certain degree of journalistic freedom, allowing her to speak openly about many usually taboo issues. For instance, in an advice column she wrote for both *Noi donne* and *Il Progresso d'Italia* she often responded to questions and concerns about such topics as unwed motherhood and marital infidelity. Most of her advice-seekers were urban working class and rural farm women, and in responding to their questions Viganò often took the Italian government and the Catholic Church to task for not meeting the needs of these women and their families.[21]

Viganò also wrote many articles about the *mondine*, a group with which she was quite familiar. Her published books include *Le mondine* (1952), a collection of personal narratives and essays previously published in *L'Unità*, and dedicated appropriately to Margotti. In *Le mondine* Viganò, speaking directly to the women workers, explains that she lived among them in order to get to know them and their work better:

> É dall'ultima settimana di maggio che sto con voi. Più di quaranta giorni che giro per le regioni del riso, che vengo a trovarvi nelle vostre case, che prendo parte alla vostra vita. (10)

> I have been with you since the last week of May. I have been traveling around the rice regions for over forty days, visiting you in your homes, and taking part in your lives.

Such first-hand experience gave rise to her active participation in their struggle to improve work and living conditions in the rice fields. In fact, much of the book is policy-oriented—Viganò was particularly interested in getting rice workers to vote, as she saw them as a voting bloc potentially able to affect labor laws.[22] The essays, then, read more like editorials than pieces of fiction or straight reportage. As a matter of fact, Viganò has a certain disdain for fictionalized accounts of the rice workers (though she does not name names):

> Mi sono accorto che sapevo ben poco. Inquadrature letterarie, descrizioni liriche, informazioni libresche: racconti e romanzi e articoli di colore. Ma la vostra vita vera non la conoscevo. (*Le mondine* 10)

> I realized that I knew very little. Literary pieces, lyrical descriptions, information from books: short stories, novels, and colorful articles. But I did not know your real life.

Her emphasis on the "real life" of workers, theoretically in line with Gramsci, seems, in fact, connected to her personal history of political activism.

Viganò had been politically active since the years leading up to World War II. Born in 1900 into a middle-class family, she led a quiet life as a nurse in her native Bologna until she met Antonio Meluschi in 1935. Meluschi, whom she would marry two years later, was a recently released political prisoner (he had spent some of his time in jail with Gramsci), and Viganò, ignoring convention, offered him a place to sleep in her apartment. The friendship that grew between them included a shared social philosophy; and, indeed, Viganò credits her Communist beliefs to Meluschi, who had introduced her to ways of thinking she had never before articulated:

> Al centro del mio supino e timoroso attaccamento al lavoro, egli [Meluschi] costruì una coscienza di classe, precisò il rapporto fra quello che ero e quello

che avrei dovuto essere, che avremmo dovuto e potuto essere, che avremmo dovuto e potuto essere tutti, e che saremo di certo in avvenire. Impiegò per questo una mia congenita predisposizione alla collettività, il fraterno amore verso i poveri che soffrono, consequente ad un mio vecchio disprezzo per la casta da cui derivavo e che avevo abbandonato con distacco polemico e scoperto. (in Colombo, *Matrimonio* 189)

At the center of my apathetic and timid attachment to work, he [Meluschi] constructed in me a sense of class consciousness, he concentrated on the relationship between what I was and what I should have been, what we should have and could have become, and that which we would all certainly become. For this he employed an innate predisposition I had to a collective nature, my fraternal love toward the poor who suffer, as well as an old hate I had for the class from which I came and which I had abandoned with an openly polemical detachment.

Viganò joined the Italian Communist Party (PCI), and when World War II broke out she became involved in the organized, anti-Fascist Resistance movement. By the final years of the war she was part of her husband's partisan unit, even bringing along their adopted son, Bu, when she was out on a mission.[23]

For Viganò, the Resistance became "la cosa più importante nelle azioni della [sua] vita" ("the single most important event in [her] life"); thus she reflects on the war and the Resistance when she turns to other topics, such as the rice worker situation (in Colombo, *Matrimonio* 95). Therefore, the dedication of *Le mondine* to Margotti, a *mondina* and a former partisan, illustrates how Margotti becomes an instant martyr for agricultural workers and labor activists, not only because she was a young, hard-working widowed mother, but also, Viganò implies, because she had been a partisan during World War II. Viganò takes Margotti's position as heroine of the agricultural worker one step further by making her a heroine for anyone who fought against Fascism. Although Margotti died as a rice worker, wearing her "fazzoletto bianco da mondina" ("white *mondina* scarf"), Viganò makes clear that she lived her life as a partisan in the never-ending battle against the state (*Le mondine* 20). In fact, Viganò explains that she first met Margotti under her battle name, Maria de fiol ed Battesta, a partisan in Mulino di Filo (between the provinces of Ravenna and Ferrara). In *Le mondine*, Viganò refers to the World War II partisan experience to illustrate the relationship between the revolutionary fight against Fascism and the rice workers' fight against the landowners. For Viganò the partisan struggle has not ended. Although she recognizes that the *carabiniere* who shot Margotti was too young to have been involved in the war, she maintains that "qualcuno di quelli che oggi lo comandano, in quei giorni [di guerra] stava nella repubblica di Salò" ("some of those men who command him today were part of the Salò Republic in those [war] days") (*Le mondine* 23). Questioning the postwar government structure, she wonders: "Davvero, mi piacerebbe sapere dove erano, durante la guerra partigiana, i comandanti del giovane carabiniere che ha ucciso la Maria Margotti di Mulino di Filo" ("Honestly, I would like to know where the commanders of that young *carabiniere* who killed Maria Margotti of Mulino di Filo were during the partisan war") (23). By speculating if the Italian State structure has changed since Fascism, Viganò, anticipating more recent scholarship, argues against a kind of history-telling that categorizes events, like Fascism, into neat packages. In other words, Fascism, Viganò insists, was not contained within the twenty-two years of Mussolini's dictatorship. Furthermore, Margotti's death is not an isolated event, an unfortunate outcome of an explicit moment of resistance. Instead her death is a visible attack by the government, and workers are subject to such attacks every year in the less-visible space of the rice paddies. Such strategic links evoke a Gramscian kind of alliance building and emphasize the role of the working class in creating a cultural counter-hegemony.

Viganò foregrounds Margotti's death as a way of reminding her readers of the unfortunate lives of many other women, and she turns Margotti into a symbol of the *mondine*'s *miseria*: thus Margotti stands for "le sue oscure compagne che . . . ogni anno nella risaia muoiono sotto i colpi della miseria nell'offensiva dell'ingiustizia; muoiono per la tremenda impossibilità di rinunciare a quei pochi soldi santi e maledetti" ("her humble sisters who die each year in the rice fields under the blows of poverty in the defense of injustice; they die because of the tremendous impossibility to do without that bit of blessed and cursed money") (*Le mondine* 13). As a result, Viganò, continuing to set up parallels between World War II and the postwar rice worker situation, names a different war: the one the Italian government fights "contro tutto il vero popolo d'Italia" ("against all of the real people of Italy"), the same people, who by means of synecdoche, Margotti represents (24). Similarly, the novelist Italo Calvino, after a visit to the various rice-growing regions, names this same war when he writes: "Molte lotte per la dignità del popolo italiano sono state combattute in risaia" ("Many battles over the dignity of the Italian people have been fought in the rice fields") (in Gualandi 60).[24] Thus Margotti stands for all the exploited people of Italy, and, similarly, the rice field becomes the site of power and conflict for those people.

As a kind of cinematic afterlife for Margotti, the character of Silvana Melega (played by Silvana Mangano), in Giuseppe De Santis's *Riso amaro* (*Bitter Rice*), emphasizes a similar battle toward the creation of a counter-hegemony grounded in women's experiences.[25] In the 1949 blockbuster, the best-known creative work about the *mondine*, Silvana, like Margotti, represents the other *mondine* and, more broadly, all female peasants.

While one would hope to find a connection between Viganò's writing on the *mondine* and De Santis's film, no explicit link has surfaced. The director's and scriptwriters' notes on the film make no allusions to Viganò, Margotti, or Colombi. The plight of the rice workers had been described in leftist newspapers, mainly because it was part of the larger national story of Italian labor, and De Santis would therefore likely have been familiar with the outline of the *mondine*'s struggle. However convenient it would be for my present argument, if De Santis was familiar with Viganò's work—or, for that matter, with any of the creative writing on *mondine*—he did not make it public, nor do the film's story and Viganò's essays offer any kind of textual similarity, except in the most general ways.

Nonetheless, the film sparked what Antonio Vitti, in his *Giuseppe De Santis*, claims is "the first national debate on a film" started by Davide Lajolo on the pages of *L'Unità* (Vitti 36). From the left, critics such as Guido Aristarco declared, "[t]he workers cannot be educated with the bare legs of Silvana" (in Vitti 36). The film was also blacklisted by the Vatican because of what were considered pornographic shots of the women's legs. The result was a box office smash that boosted the unknown Mangano to international stardom and inadvertently reinstated the star system in the Italian film industry. De Santis and his collaborators won an Oscar nomination for best original story, but the director was not allowed to enter the United States because of his ties to the PCI. The fact that a critical debate exists about the film would seem at odds with the notion that the *mondine* have been ignored; however, much of the hostile criticism of the film has focused on its style rather than the female labor it represents—because it succumbs to Hollywood-style glamour, critics argue, *Riso amaro* loses any potential to carry a social message.[26]

The film also depicts the forty days of the *mondatura*, the rice weeding season, and its narrative unfolds across a variety of cinematic genres, borrowing elements from the documentary, melodrama, neorealist, and Hollywood gangster pictures. The real historical Margotti was killed by the state; the fictional Silvana is raped by a convict and we as viewers are pushed to take part visually in that rape. While Margotti's retribution lies in the hands of her comrades who continued to fight for their rights, Silvana takes retribution into her own hands—killing her rapist before she takes her own life, unable to see any other options. Her rape comes to signify not only a defilement of her body but of all the *mondine*; it also comments on the capitalist exploitation of the land. Thus her retribution becomes a form of resistance in the name of all the women workers and in the name of the land itself. The film concludes with all the women throwing their hard-earned rice on the still body of Silvana, marking the kind of alliance formation Gramsci called for, an alliance that came at the bitter expense of Silvana's own life.[27] Silvana's symbolic death therefore parallels Calvino's and Viganò's separate assertions that symbolically link the *mondine* to all underrepresented people.

End of the Rice Season

In a parliamentary discussion held in 1903 and published by the Italian government in a pamphlet called *Alle risaiole* (*In the Rice Fields*), Senator Cabrini stated: "La stessa arte, che suole determinare negli spiriti gentili le piu profonde emozioni, la stessa arte protesta, in nome della umanita" ("The same art that normally awakens, in the most gentle spirits, deep emotion, that same art protests in the name of humanity") (7). Cabrini referred specifically to artistic productions featuring *mondine*, in particular Marchesa Colombi's novel, *In risaia*. The novel, published in 1878, remains out of print. Lucienne Kroha, in *The Woman Writer in Late-Nineteenth Century Italy: Gender and the Formation of Literary Identity*, only mentions the novel in passing, highlighting Cabrini's main point. She explains: "Though entirely forgettable at the literary level, *In risaia* did attract considerable attention at the time of publication because of its implicit plea for better working conditions for the poor" (48).[28] What Cabrini and Kroha both suggest is that Colombi's novel forms a kind of national popular culture (what Kroha calls, evoking U.S. writers like John Steinbeck, perhaps, a "socially-conscious" novel) based on the experiences of subalterns and thus able to question women's social conditions.

Gramsci's writing emphasizes the possibility of forming a counterhegemony through folk culture, a resistance-oriented mode of artistic expression that could contribute to the development of a national popular culture. Such possibilities are brought to light in the contemporary moment through the songs and performances of groups like the *Coro delle mondine*. They link their quotidian labor experiences to landmark labor experiences, such as the death of Maria Margotti, and appeal to a greater audience through the medium of popular song. Similarly, Viganò's personal essays attempt to place the rice workers into an historical trajectory that includes those moments of Italy's past (e.g., World War II) with which her readers would have been more familiar, thus forming a cultural text in which many could participate. Although Viganò's works remain in the shadow of better-known texts, the potential to have her writing be part of a national popular culture remains. The experiences of the *mondine*, recorded in a variety of textual artifacts and viewed through the lens of contemporary cultural studies, helps us reimagine the participation of Italian women within Italian national history and thus within the formation of a counter-hegemonic national popular culture.

Notes

1. "If you don't recognize us/Look us in the eyes/we are the sisters of Maria Margotti" (in Gualandi 68).
2. *Mondina* is the popular word for a "woman rice weeder" and is also used generally to mean "woman rice worker."
3. See Candelora, Vol 11 (208–218), on the 1940s strikes, specifically page 213 for a discussion of the 1949 strike.
4. Cgil stands for the "Italian General Confederation of Labor." The eulogy reads:

> May 17, 1949: All of Italy's farm laborers have already been striking for a few days, striking against poverty and exploitation by the landowners. The *mondine* of the Po Valley are in the front ranks, the landowners attempt to stem the forces by organizing scabs. The *mondine* confront the scabs, speak with them, and convince them to return to their homes in the mountains.
>
> In Molinella there are five women on an embankment near the road: a motorcycle passes by, a voice orders the women to leave. Then a shot is heard, one of the women falls. Maria Margotti dies, a thirty-four-year-old woman, six years a widow, who, with her exhausting work as a *mondina* has raised her daughters. A woman heroically dies, a woman who, along with her female comrades, was only trying to defend her right to work, her right to give bread to her two daughters.
>
> Today, in her name, all of the *mondine* of Italy continue their battles to defend those rights for which Maria Margotti sacrificed her young life.

5. Most major histories of Italy do not consider the *mondine* as a unique category of workers; see Candelora's *Storia dell'italia moderna*, Spencer Di Scala's *Italy: From Revolution to Republic*, and Roger Absalom's *Italy Since 1800*.
6. Those three studies are Elda Gentili Zappi's *If Eight Hours Seem Too Few* (1991); Irea Gualandi's *Tra cronaca, storia, e testimonianza* (1984); and Marco Paterlini's *Quando saremo a Reggio Emilia* (1987). Zappi's text is a U.S.-published book, readily available in university libraries; the other two books are not: I came across Gualandi's in the Gramsci Institute in Bologna, and Paterlini's was sent to me by the Library of the City of Correggio in Reggio Emilia when I contacted them about the Correggio-based singing group, Coro delle mondine. Unless otherwise noted, my historical references to the rice workers come from these three books.

7. Franca Pieroni Bortolotti devotes a chapter to the PSI *leghe* in *Socialismo e questione femminile*. Although she does not specifically discuss the Po *leghe*, she does examine what progress these groups made for women's emancipation and thus illustrates a noteworthy aspect of the Socialist Party (with respect to women).

8. Women left behind by migrating men were not only offered a new kind of independence, they sometimes also led better lives than their husbands who were struggling in the various "New Worlds." Ann Cornelisen in her interviews and narrative of southern Italian women offers us two late twentieth-century perspectives of southern women whose husbands had gone north for work. These opinions illustrate the different effects of migration. First there is Ninetta, who wants desperately to migrate north with her husband; he wants her to remain in their village: "If he doesn't want me to come . . . I'll go somewhere else and work for all of us. I'm through here. I can't take it anymore. Can you understand what I mean? Do you understand why I can't take anymore? Do you?" (92). On the other side is Teresa, whose husband was not particularly successful in his search for stable work in the north. Nevertheless, she wanted him to continue trying while she stayed put:

> Maybe I should have gone with him, but they wouldn't have let him be home much, and I had to pay rent and no one knows me. I saw it much different and I still do. To me my job is to see this land gets farmed, to raise the children, make them go to school and teach them what's right and get as much work as I can get while I'm still young enough to work in the fields, because that's all I know. (123)

9. On the Vercelli strike see Zappi (158–172).

10. Another description of the *mondine*'s anti-Fascist protests is to be found in Remigio Barbieri's "Mondine di Medicina." I will note here the one, as-of-yet unmentioned, critical consideration of the *mondine*: Annarella Quasi's article on turn-of-the-century *mondine* labor movements in Vercelli.

11. Scholarly nods to the rice workers (in relation to Colombi's writings) can be found in Donald Meyer (450), Lucienne Kroha (48–49), and Maria Teresa Cometto.

12. Gramsci briefly discusses Ada Negri in his notebooks calling for more study of her work and life and suggesting that she be considered either a "'poetessa proletaria' o semplicemente 'popolare'" ("'a proletariat poet' or simply a 'popular one'") (*Letteratura e vita nazionale* 165).

13. Many examples of visual artists' renditions of the rice workers are to be found in Viganò's *Le mondine*. Those artists are Borgonzoni, Guttuso, Maccini, Sughi, Treccani, and Vespignani. Other paintings and photographs of the *mondine* can easily be viewed on the Internet.

14. Colombi's novel can perhaps be considered "self-representation" in that it was only because of her strong will and mere good fortune that she did not become a rice worker, or so hypothesizes the journalist Cometto in her 1996 narrative biography about Colombi.

15. "In the morning, just after waking/ To the rice fields, I must go./And among insects and mosquitoes,/much hard work I must do."

16. "Oh partisan, take me away, because I feel like I'm going to die."

17. There are mixed views of the song's conception. Giovanna Daffini, a former *mondina* interviewed in the 1960s, recalls learning the song in the rice fields either in Vercelli around 1932–1933 or in Novara in 1940. Either would imply that the Resistance version of the song came second. Meanwhile, Vasco Scansance, a former rice worker—one of few men who weeded—claims to have authored the song after World War II and to have based it on the already existing Resistance song (Gualandi).

18. Agnese's job as a washerwoman is central to her development into a partisan who has achieved class consciousness. For instance, her job is connected to the manner in which she kills the German soldier and the way the narrator describes the act: Agnese takes the gun and bashes it on the man's head, "come quando sbatteva sull'asse del lavatoio i pesanti lenzuoli matrimoniali" ("like when she hit the large heavy sheets on the washing stone") (Viganò, *L'Agnese* 54). For a literary analysis of Agnese's *contadina*-style resistance see my "La contadina si ribella."

19. Only Viganò's Resistance novel, *L'Agnese va a morire*, is still in print today, frequently anthologized for Italian high school textbooks and studied in relation to other World War II Italian literature. Her other writings have been virtually ignored and have fallen into a cultural abyss that is not too uncommon for Italian women writers. Her prose style, informed by her explicit and sometimes rigidly dogmatic political positions, likely plays a role in Viganò's relative obscurity as well.

20. Viganò's published works include *L'Agnese va a morire* (1949), *Le mondine* (1952), *Arriva la cicogna* (1954), *Donne della resistenza* (1955), *Ho conosciuto Ciro* (1959), *Una storia di ragazze* (1962), and the posthumous *Matrimonio in brigata* (1976).

21. For a critical review of Viganò's journalistic writings (including her advice letters), see Giancarla Codrignani's "Quando ignoravamo la questione di genere" (in Colombo).

22. Italian women gained the vote in 1945, but all eligible voters did not immediately take advantage of their right.

23. For more biographical details about Meluschi and Viganò see the catalog of the 1995 museum show, *Matrimonio in brigata* (edited by Enzo Colombo).

24. Calvino wrote about the *mondine* for the PCI-funded publication, *La risaia*, in 1950. Throughout the years there have been a variety of publications written for and about the rice workers, most were funded by political parties and union organizers, such as the Fascists' *Mondina* and the Cgil's *Per te mondina*.

25. Much has been made of De Santis's Gramscian approach to filmmaking (see Vitti and Marcus), but by 1948, when *Riso amaro* was made, only sections of Gramsci's prison letters had been published. These early letters do not much expand upon Gramsci's more critical thoughts on the role of intellectuals or the role of the Risorgimento in the so-called Southern Question, ideas that might, had they been made known earlier, seem to inform this film. This is not to say, though, that one cannot easily see De Santis as a Gramscian filmmaker, but that the influence is most likely not direct, flowing rather from the Italian leftist intellectual circles that informed De

Santis's development as an artist. See Carlo Lizzani (25) for a brief discussion of how familiar De Santis was with Gramsci when the former made *Riso amaro*. For further discussion of Gramsci and cinema more generally, see Landy, Verdicchio (*Bound by Distance*), and Ruberto and Wilson (*Italian Neorealism and Global Cinema*).

26. Elsewhere I critique this position and instead read the film as strategically disrupting the Italian neorealist paradigm, which relied on relationships between men, by its unique representation of strong working women (see my *Producing Culture*).

27. The only man who stands with the *mondine* as they encircle the dead Silvana is Marco, who has acted as a kind of heavy-handed, organic intellectual, guiding the women in their labor actions. Marco's character also reminds us of the lack of prosperity in postwar Italy and the ultimate limitations of any alliance formation since he has made plans to emigrate to Argentina, a place he romanticizes as a "paese vergine" ("virgin country").

28. Kroha earlier explains that it is only because of Italo Calvino and Natalia Ginzburg that Colombi's writing has not entirely "passed into oblivion" (47), as it was Ginzburg who introduced Calvino to Colombi's novel *Un matriomonio in provincia*, and who, in turn, persuaded Einuadi to reprint it in 1973.

CHAPTER TWO

Migrant Domestic Labor and the Creation of Identity

Domestic-Servant-Style Tomatoes

Don't pick tomatoes that are too ripe. Cut them in half, remove the seeds, and let them drain until they naturally rid themselves of their liquid. Lay them in a baking pan and spread over:
  a clove of chopped garlic;
  oregano;
  a sprig of parsley;
  salt;
  pepper;
  grated parmesan;
  30 grams of oil.
Place the baking pan in the oven until they are golden-colored.

—Petronius, *Ricettario della felicità*, 195

The paid domestic worker holds a unique position inside the house of her employer. Required to listen and labor in a space isolated from other domestics, she is one of the more silenced kinds of workers. For Wanda Tommasi of Milan's Feminist *Diotima Community*, domestic servants are an example of workers "ridotti al silenzio" ("reduced to silence") (in Cigarini 126) because of the conditions of their employment. For such workers, "prendere la parola" (literally, "to take the word"), that is, breaking the silence, can be accomplished in many ways, some direct and practical, such as organizing and protesting work conditions, others less directly beneficial and almost symbolic in nature. Such symbolic gestures are often accomplished through creative representations, like testimonials or stories, which describe their labor to an outside audience. As Tommasi explains:

> Dare voce alla propria esperienza al di fuori di modelli linquistico-comunicativi codificati; può voler dire, ad esempio, descrivere la sequenza di operazioni necessarie per confezionare una giacca, mettendo in rilievo gli inciampi, le decisioni che occorre prendere, i vissuti. (in Cigarini 126)

> To give voice to one's experience outside of codified linguistic-communicative models, can mean, for example, to describe the sequence of operation that is necessary to package a jacket, highlighting the obstacles, the decisions one makes, all lived experiences.

Such disclosures, Tommasi argues, demystify domestic labor by identifying all its intricacies and, in so doing, act to liberate the worker.

In her essay, "Il lavoro tra necessità e libertà," Tommasi, distinguishing between a middle-class, Western, privileged position and a working-class and/or nonwestern position, considers how and for whom work can be liberating.[1] She contemplates ways women can free themselves from traditional, Western conceptions of labor, notions that deem the production (and reproduction) performed by women degrading, inconsequential, and worthless. In a sense Tommasi's call parallels Gramsci's recognition of the relationship between waged labor, unwaged labor, and sexuality. Further, Tommasi's contemporary emphasis on the cultural power of gender-specific work (such as domestic labor) is in line with Gramsci's perspective that subalterns can be producers of culture.

Tommasi ends with an open-ended call for a change in the symbolic value afforded certain kinds of labor, noting domestic labor, in particular. An imbalance exists, she explains, between certain professions that are related, albeit in different ways, to helping people. Using the example of medical doctors and domestic workers, she notes the high monetary and symbolic value given medical doctors versus the low value given to domestic work. This disparity is illogical, Tommasi contends, because domestic work offers "mediazioni alla vita immediata" ("mediation to real life") (in Cigarini 133). That is, domestic work creates a direct and intimate relationship with the everyday cultural practices and experiences of a family. She goes on to describe paid domestic labor as "un'opera di civiltà nel senso più alto perché, a partire dai bisogni, nominati come tali, senza abbellimenti, fanno ordine, senso, mondo" ("a work of civilization in the highest sense, because, beyond fulfilling needs, named such without embellishment, they make order, offer direction, they make the world") (in Cigarini 133). She then concludes by calling for an adjustment to this imbalance so that domestic work is not only equal to other labor but valued even more highly—so that workers, like domestic servants, who create and sustain the culture of everyday life are given credit for their labor:

> Collocarli al centro significa rimettere in ordine quello squilibrio simbolico che . . . [il] denaro come unica misura del valore non è riuscita a correggere, semmai ad aggravare. (in Cigarini 133)
>
> To place them in the center signifies reorganizing that symbolic imbalance that . . . money as the only measure of value has not been able to correct, and in fact has aggravated.

As Tommasi suggests, domestic servants, in their connection to the everyday practices within a home, are important to the formation of dominant notions of culture. At the same time their mere existence points to a (potential national popular) culture that counters the dominant culture. In other words, by recognizing domestic work as "a work of civilization" (in Cigarini 133), Tommasi links such labor to the production of culture, and thus makes a Gramscian move, recognizing the need to analyze the seemingly private domestic space in relation to the seemingly public market space. By extension, cultural representations of domestic servants in Italy illustrate how the figure of the domestic servant in part makes possible the construction of a bourgeois, middle-class Italian culture and sometimes alters or challenges that same middle-class culture. Put still another way, domestic workers have the potential to create a national popular culture that counters the hegemonic structure while at the same time sustaining the hegemony of the nation-state.

The creation of a dominant, middle-class culture has deep roots in the seemingly private sphere of the home. Gramsci recognizes this when he noted the role of sexuality in his discussion of Fordism, but feminist theory has developed the critique further. Much feminist criticism has argued that the middle-class housewife, through her caregiver role—consider the nineteenth-century image of the domestic saint—guides and supports such nation-based identity-building. However, the existence of waged domestic labor takes this relationship one step further by recognizing that the caregiver role can in part be performed by other nonfamilial members of the household (from slaves to waged domestic workers). Thus the seemingly balanced and well-structured formation of national middle-class identity (based on certain prescribed ideas about the role of bourgeois men and women in society) is disrupted when we stop to consider the role of the working class and, in this instance, of domestic workers.[2]

The domestic worker, who in Italy has predominantly been female since the eighteenth century, occupies both the domestic, private sphere and the public, market sphere. The domestic sphere is directly thrown into the marketplace by the existence of paid domestic labor, a form of employment that breaks apart any remaining sense of a strict division between private and public sphere. Thus we may find subaltern alternatives in the internal space of the home. In other words, because of the commodification of domesticity inherent in paid domestic labor, it "provides," as Mary Romero suggests, "a window into the relationship of housework to the economy per se" (31).

As such, this chapter considers various representations of Italian domestic servants covering roughly the last half of the twentieth century in order to explore the relationship between migration, domestic work, gender, and the creation of alternatives to the culture supported by the hegemony of the nation-state. Such a temporal breadth allows us to see the Italian domestic servant in the early to mid-twentieth-century as generally a young single woman migrating to a northern Italian city from economically depressed rural areas (northern or southern); in more recent years, instead, many married women (and some men) from beyond Western Europe take on such work. The texts examined include, recipes in Petronius's *Ricettario della felicità* (*Cookbook of Happiness*), (1961), Renata Viganò's novel, *Una storia di ragazze* (*A Story about Girls*), (1962), and two collections of testimonials by Italian immigrant women (1991's *La terra in faccia* [*Dirt in the Face*] and 1992's *Ho trovato l'occidente* [*I Found the Occident*]). Such an analysis takes to heart what Romero explains as one of the unique qualities of the domestic worker situation. She notes that

> domestic service is a unique social setting in which to explore relationships between women. Rarely in our society do women (or men) from different social-economic, racial, and ethnic backgrounds interact in an informal and intimate setting. The employer's home, in which domestics and employers interact brings several important factors to bear simultaneously: shared gender, interracial and interclass oppression, and location within women's primary unrecognized workplace—the household. (119)

Accordingly, a critical look at varied cultural representations of domestic workers in Italy is quintessentially Gramscian.

Gramsci recognized the relevance of everyday practices, or what he more specifically called folklore, in relation to subablterns' ability to create a counter-hegemony. Thus to consider the relationship between domestic workers' experiences (the subalterns' everyday practices) and domestic workers' influence on middle-class culture (the subalterns' contribution to both a hegemony and counter-hegemony) makes sense. His analysis of common sense plays into this relationship as it suggests the possibility of a complex recognition of an individual's position even as it is defined against his more worldly notion of good sense. As Landy suggests (and as I set out in the introduction to this book), common sense can be understood as a recognition of "various strata of philosophy, religion, institutional practices, and individual experiences" (78). Further, he understood a powerful relationship between what happens within feminine domesticized spaces and what happens beyond those spaces, namely, in the factory and public market arenas. Thus Gramsci might illuminate ways disenfranchised women workers produce alternatives to hegemonic culture (even as they may simultaneously reaffirm that same dominant culture) through their everyday practices, folklore, language, relationship to organic intellectuals, and possible alliances with other disenfranchised groups. Finally, in line with other examples, when we consider the case of contemporary immigrant domestic workers in Italy, Gramsci's idea of a national popular culture loses its edge, and instead an international popular culture must take its place.

With different levels of success, the cultural texts I discuss presently characterize the possibility of a national (or international) popular culture built in part on the labor and cultural representation of domestic workers. Some of the texts illustrate how common sense or cross-subaltern alliances could be applied to create an alternative to the hegemonic culture. However such efforts are not always possible in the real world of women workers. In fact, a distinction needs to be made between the texts as examples of culture being created in the name of subaltern classes and the individuals represented, who do not necessarily support or succeed in the creation of such culture. That said, some of the texts discussed in this chapter—in particular the 1990s testimonials of recent immigrants to Italy—demonstrate the possibility of a subaltern alternative to the hegemonic culture of the nation-state. In other words, Gramsci was right to the extent that future solidarities and the creation of national popular culture might be carved out of existing divisions. That he was looking internally at the prospects of the subalterns acting alone in one nation is an instance of historically specific myopia, but one that does not obviate the possibility of applying his ideas to a more global sense of "national" (or, indeed an international) popular culture.

The Role of Migration in Domestic Worker History

Scholarship on domestic workers strives to make this category of workers visible in the realm of academic discourse.[3] Within Italian studies, discussions of domestic workers form a central aspect of many historical analyses of gender and class in pre-twentieth-century eras. Much of this research focuses on the domestic worker ("maid" or "servant") with respect to the rise of the middle class in Italian urban societies. For instance, Raffaella Sarti's work on domestic worker labor manuals from the sixteenth century traces, among other things, the contradictory representations of a servant woman, Saint Zita, while elsewhere Sarti explains how the feminization of domestic labor in the eighteenth century corresponds to a devaluing of such labor. Margherita Di Fazio Alberti proceeds in a more literary direction by investigating representations of servants in early nineteenth-century Italian literature, focusing, in particular, on a stylistic analysis of Alessandro Manzoni's *I promessi sposi*. Maura Palazzi's studies, which revolve around the experiences of laboring women in different eras, are useful for keeping track of the wide variety of labor women performed (paid and unpaid). In "L'Emigrazione al femminile," Palazzi explains the history of domestic work in Emilia Romagna; this northern Italian example illustrates some of the historical changes of domestic work in Italy:

> Il servizio domestico costituisce un settore di attività che si è femminilizzato nel corso dell'Ottocento, quando l'avvio del processo di industrializzazione ha aperto agli uomini nuove possibilità d'impiego. Una larga componente dell'occupazione in tale attività era alimentata a quell'epoca dalle donne emigrate dalle campagne. . . . Nel corso del Novecento e soprattutto dopo la seconda guerra mondiale . . . [l]e donne emigrate dalle campagne circostanti erano ormai assorbite in attività manifatturiere o del terziario, mentre il servizio domestico era soprattutto riservato all'emigrazione femminile proveniente dalle aree depresse dell'Italia come il Veneto, il Meridione, la Sardegna. . . . [n]egli anni Settanta . . . [i]l sevizio domestico a tempo pieno è cominciato a divenire un settore in cui era impiegata prevalentemente manodopera femminile immigrata dall'estero. (22–23)

> Domestic service forms a service sector which became feminized during the eighteenth century, when the start of the process of industrialization opened up new possibilities of employment for men. At that time, a large portion of work in this area was fueled by women who emigrated from the countryside. . . . During the nineteenth century, and above all after the Second World War . . . women who had emigrated from the nearby countryside had been absorbed in manufacturing or in tertiary activities, while domestic service was reserved,

above all, to female emigration from the economically depressed areas of Italy, like the Veneto region, the Southern regions, and Sardegna. . . . in the Seventies . . . full time domestic service began to become a sector in which for the most part foreign female immigrants were employed.

Recognizing different kinds of migration in different historical moments allows us to illuminate, for one, the effect of the growing global economy on specific groups of workers. Under capitalism, the middle class secures its identity through the working class, and in particular the labor of domestic workers helps constitute this identity. As globalization develops, the Italian working class changes to include more foreign-born workers, and the culture of the nation-state often excludes those foreign-born domestic workers.

The Kitchen as Public Space

In the 1961 cookbook, *Ricettario della felicità* (*Cookbook of Happiness*), written expressly for the "padrona di casa" ("lady of the house") the domestic servant's relationship to Italian middle-class culture is established by such easy-to-prepare dishes as the oven-baked domestic servant–style tomatoes, noted in this chapter's epigraph. While something as transparent as a cookbook seems like an unlikely text to mark as representative of a theoretical position, such a text can be at the very least fruitful in preliminary thoughts on the topic of domestic workers' relationship to their employers. More specifically, the kitchen and the primary written text connected to it, the cookbook (a text that by definition holds information about, and representations of, domestic work) can act as a window to a more grounded discussion of how domestic servitude lies somewhere between the private home environment and the public market space. Furthermore, similar to Tommasi's idea about domestic work as a "work of civilization," this particular cookbook demonstrates how paid domestic workers help produce and sustain a certain culture in which they are not allowed to participate—thus calling attention to domestic workers varied relationship to hegemonic culture.

The *Ricettario della felicità* has directions for dishes from all parts of the Mediterranean boot, such as gnocchi alla Romana, tonno alla Siciliana, and tortellini alla Bolognese. It also contains two recipes attributed to domestic servants; the one quoted above, and manzo alla domestica (domestic servant potroast), not to be confused with the more complicated dish, manzo alla casalinga (housewife potroast). The recipe for housewife-style potroast mixes together onions, carrots, celery, dried mushrooms, prosciutto, and bay leaf and suggests adding a hint of marsala at the end. The recipe also instructs the cook on how the roast should be presented, a step left out of the domestic worker–inspired recipes: "Al momento di servire passate il sugo formatosi nella casseruola e lasciatelo cadere sulla carne che avrete deposta in un piatto da portata" ("Right before serving strain the sauce which has formed in the pot and pour it over the meat, which you have placed in a serving platter") (161). The domestic servant version of a potroast, instead, is a much simpler dish that calls for simmering together pieces of beef with onions, tomatoes, and potatoes. The recipe has no suggestion for presentation and advises very plainly to cook and serve: "Lasciate cuocere ancora per un'oretta poi potete servire" ("Let it cook for another hour and then you can serve it") (157). Like the tomato dish, its preparation is very basic and perfect for a woman with little time on her hands for cooking.[4]

What can these recipes tell us about paid domestic labor in Italy? We might begin by inquiring why the recipes were given those names. Were the domestic servant recipes so named because they were common dishes prepared by all domestic servants or because they are simple dishes, perfect for a new kind of woman on the go, easily prepared with ingredients that would be in all Italian kitchens? The existence of these two domestic servant–inspired dishes in a cookbook for housewives confuses the issue of domestic chores, for it assumes that the housewife reading the book does not have a domestic servant who will do the cooking for her, at least not on a daily basis. That the housewife would whip up meals associated in some way with "hired help" suggests that the book was arranged in such a way as to establish domestic servitude in the housewife's own culture. The inside jacket cover, the only form of an introduction the book has, claims that these recipes will help the housewife "mantenere viva e calda la fiamma del focolare domestico" ("maintain a lively and warm flame in the domestic hearth"). Thus paid domestic labor has a part in the creation and preservation of a homey environment for others. The housewife who cooks and serves a domestic servant–style meal can distance herself, at least through the name of the dish, from the labor involved in the preparation of the food. In other words, she plays the role of the servant by cooking the simple dish, but her seemingly privileged position as a housewife (an unwaged worker) detaches her from that otherwise laborious role. Moreover, her detachment is further established by her ability to choose to cook the simple meal or the more elaborate housewife meal. Distancing herself from certain homemaking chores, she can play the role of the paid domestic servant (by cooking and serving the simpler recipes) without identifying with that labor, and thus she reinforces her own middle-class position. The choices the housewife has are products of her middle-class status, benefits the domestic worker does not have; the housewife can imagine herself as someone who has a domestic worker. That is, the housewife can reaffirm her own importance by making a simpler recipe, the assumption being that even if the domestic worker had time to prepare the more complicated "housewife" dish she would not have the skill to do so.

A seemingly transparent recipe thus unveils complexities about the relationship between domestic servants (and the representation of their labor) and dominant, middle-class Italian culture. Focusing on the Italian case, we can see some of the ways domestic servants had and continue to have a part in the formation of what we can generally call Italian culture (think only of the relationship between food and the creation of culture within the cookbook). Their relationship to that culture remains paradoxical: On the one hand they are sometimes part of its formation; on the other hand they are often excluded from its middle-class privileges, either linguistically, culturally, racially, or by some combination of those factors. Nonetheless, a meal cooked by a housewife but named after domestic servants functions to mark domestic servant's contribution to the housewife's bourgeois culture. Thus recipes named for domestic labor suggest the complex way in which domestic workers, and by consequence their bosses, inhabit spheres that are often deemed separate and distinct, public and private.

In fact, the modern division of Western society into public and private spheres, corresponding, respectively, to masculine and feminine spheres, already shown by cultural critics to be imagined and sustained by a variety of interrelated cultural apparati, becomes further unsettled when we consider the situation of domestic workers. Many interventions have been made regarding Jurgen Habermas's influential study of the nineteenth-century development of the European liberal public sphere alongside the development of industrial capitalism. For instance, Nancy Fraser theorizes the public sphere in a more complex manner, rejecting both a strict binary of public and private and problematizing Habermas's idealization of a single liberal public sphere. Although Fraser points out that Habermas recognizes other public spheres, he "assumes that it is possible to understand the character of the bourgeois public by looking at it alone;" instead, she explains how "the view that women were excluded from the public sphere turns out to be ideological; it rests on a class- and gender-biased notion of publicity, one which accepts at face value the bourgeois public's claim to be *the* public" (Fraser 78 and 61; emphasis in original). Thus she proposes alternative public spheres, or invoking Gramsci, "subaltern counterpublics" (67). These spheres are "parallel discursive arenas where members of subordinated social groups invent and circulate counter discourses, which in turn permit them to formulate oppositional interpretations of their identities, interests and needs" (67).

By seeing that the public sphere comes in many shapes and sizes, we can envision how various marginalized groups have the possibility of interacting with and influencing dominant discourse:

> On the one hand, they [subaltern counterpublics] function as spaces of withdrawal and regroupment; on the other hand, they also function as bases and training grounds for agitational activities directed toward wider publics. It is precisely in the dialectic between these two functions that their emancipatory potential resides. This dialectic enables subaltern counterpublics partially to offset, although not wholly to eradicate, the unjust participatory privileges enjoyed by members of dominant social groups in stratified societies. (68)

Fraser articulates the potential for a subaltern counter-hegemony through a reconceptualization of the public sphere. Domestic work further encourages a recognition of the idea that the spheres are politically and economically sustained and that they influence one another even when they appear not to.

In short, the domestic servant (especially one who lives at her place of employment) inhabits the slippery space between public and private. Although the domestic sphere is traditionally considered a female space, for the female domestic worker that space becomes foreign, and she lives and works marginalized within it. This situation marks the domestic servant as a decidedly interesting category of worker, because of the way her paid work space surrounds any private space she may also have within the home of her employer. She then exists in an in-between, detached identity, an identity formed by her relationship to a commodified, foreign, yet all the while domestic space.

Viganò's Domestic Worker, a Plurality of Voices

The character of the domestic worker is found in various creative pieces of the Italian postwar period, often used to accent another character's situation or as a point of comparison, rather than a central figure in the narrative (think of Maria in Vittorio De Sica's 1952 neorealist film, *Umberto D* or Giuliana in Natalia Ginzburg's 1965 play *Ti ho sposato per allegria*). Such a configuration reinforces the all-too-common marginalization of women workers, and, for the present argument, of domestic workers, both in the real world of their employment and within the representational world of culture. In contrast, Renata Vigano's 1962 novel, *Una storia di ragazze* (*A Story About Girls*) focuses on the life of a single woman domestic servant, making her situation paramount. The figure of the domestic worker in Vigano's novel functions then to critique bourgeois institutions and values and thus offer a possibility of an alternative cultural hegemony.

As discussed in chapter one, Viganò, through her writing and political activism, tried to make visible women rice worker's labor and to help the women improve their working conditions. In addition to her work with *mondine*, Viganò took an interest in the plight of Italian female domestic workers, and in so doing helped expose a type of labor and a group of women often left to fend for themselves isolated behind closed doors.[5] In a 1953 weekly "Dear Abby"-style column written for *Noi donne*, she mentions a project she was working on about domestic workers in Italy.[6] It is not surprising, then, that in 1962 she would publish *Una storia di ragazze*, a now-forgotten novel chronicling the life of a nineteen-year-old country woman who moves to Bologna, Viganò's hometown, in order to help support her family back home through her job as a maid.[7] The partially omniscient narrator follows the plight of Miranda as she becomes the live-in maid of the Serrazani family—a hard-edged mother (la Signora Irma), a soft-spoken father (il Signor Michele), a lazy brother (Ruggero), and a frivolous daughter (Piera).

By focusing on the life of Miranda, Viganò exposes the false division between public and private. Further, by narrating Miranda's inability to form a friendship with her employer's daughter, Piera, Viganò demonstrates the failure of cross-class alliances. This failed sisterhood, in turn, permits Viganò to expose certain commonly invisible societal concerns, such as abortion and unwed motherhood. These issues are tightly wound up in Miranda's relationship to middle-class culture. At its barest, *Una storia di ragazze* is exactly what the title states—a chronicle of female stories and points of view, held together by Miranda's entrance into the Serrazani home. Viganò's novel describes Miranda's everyday labors, work that helps create and sustain the Serrazani's middle-class culture; her story thus disrupts hegemonic culture generally.

While Miranda is clearly the protagonist and the character with whom the reader is led to sympathize, the narrator underscores the young women's parallel situations through the creation of a kind of cinematic screen version of Piera and Miranda: "Tutte e due erano ragazze con l'innamorato: ognuna protagonista della propria avventura, prima attrice nel film della sua vita" ("They were both girls with lovers: each a protagonist in her own adventure, the leading lady in a film about her life") (50). Miranda and Piera have parallel lives but only interact equally outside the confines of the house when they leave together after having lied to Piera's mother in order to spend time with their respective boyfriends. In fact, their friendly relationship literally ends at the front door of the Serrazani home:

> E tutto finì lì: perché arrivarono al portone di casa, e quello era il limite in cui la Miranda cessava di essere per la Piera la necessaria confidente e complice di uscite clandestine, e ridiventava la ragazza di servizio. (50)

> And everything ended there: because they reached the front door of the house, and that was the point at which Miranda stopped being Piera's necessary confidant and accomplice in their clandestine escapes, and re-became the servant girl.

The door physically signifies the socioeconomic distance between Piera and Miranda, a distance that not even similar romantic problems can reduce. Miranda is caught in the unsettling position of being a live-in domestic servant who has little personal space and privacy. Living under her employer's roof means that not even the conventionally feminine domestic space is hers. She never feels quite at home in the Serrazani house, not even in the kitchen. Signora Irma keeps such a close watch over her that she even feels as though she is being watched while working or eating in the kitchen. As Romero has noted, "although domestics are expected to create and to respect the private space of employers and their families, they themselves are denied privacy" (117). Such treatment, Romero outlines, is constructed through the language used by the employer toward the domestic, the lack of private space allotted to the domestic, and it "is also constructed through eating arrangements" (118). In her fictional account, Viganò brings into focus Romero's sociologically based comments: Miranda can only eat in the kitchen, after she has served the family, and can only eat leftovers. Moreover, Signora Irma gives her a spoon "tanto consumato che vi si era formato un piccolo buco" ("so old that a small hole had formed") (21)—such a distinction can be seen, as Romero might say, as a "way to create symbols of her [Miranda's] inferiority" (118). In a sense her employer's house becomes transformed into a Benthanite panopticon, the oppressive prison structure so usefully theorized by Foucault. Thus the only space where Miranda is not under surveillance, a space that feels like home, is outside of the front door, on the streets at the local markets, where the neighborhood merchants joke with her:

> E nelle botteghe le facevano complimenti: degli scherzi benevoli, allusioni un po' grasse, ma non offensive, e i discorsi assomigliavano a quelli degli uomini del suo paese. . . . [L]'ora della spesa diventava quasi piacevole. (53)

> And in the shops they would complement her: well-meaning jokes, slightly rude allusions, but never offensive, and the conversations were similar to those of the men of her village . . . shopping became almost enjoyable.

Thus, it is on the street that she feels most comfortable and has, at the very least, the possibility to build a real friendship with Piera.

However, Miranda and Piera's socioeconomic division, worsened by the constant reminder of Miranda's domestic worker status, makes any form of true friendship or solidarity impossible. The circumstances surrounding each of their pregnancies forms the most compelling parallel between the two characters, and one through which we come to realize how irreparably separate their identities really are. In short, normative heterosexual relationships—and the results of those relationships—come before female solidarity or friendship. When Piera becomes pregnant by her boyfriend, Mario, whom her parents do not approve of, her parents pay for an illegal abortion. (In Italy abortion was legalized in 1978.) At the time Miranda sympathetically takes care of Piera, without passing judgment; later, she comes to think of abortion as wrong. After a brief vacation, Piera seems more serene, and takes to attending church daily, "vestita di scuro" ("dressed in black") (81). In effect, her life improves after the abortion, and Miranda even notices changes in Piera's mother, "ogni tanto sorrideva" ("occasionally she would smile") (81). The class and cultural differences between Miranda and Piera make it clear that when Miranda also becomes pregnant, later in the novel, her situation will be much more complicated.

In relation to work, the two also have different experiences related to their class standing. While Piera smoothly enters the workforce, Miranda remains uncomfortable in her urban work environment. She seeks help from another maid, Olga, the closest connection she has to her old community. This affinity with Olga further validates the notion that both Miranda and Piera can only form lasting relationships with women who share their own cultural backgrounds, backgrounds that are intricately linked to a sense of class status as well as economic stability. With the help of her old acquaintance, Miranda finds another place to live and a better paying job as a washerwoman for a butcher shop. Her ties to Piera and the rest of the Serrazani family are completely broken. The relationship they had was, in fact, one-sided and was sustained by the employer-employee dichotomy. Piera seems unable to recognize the reciprocal benefits she and Miranda might gain if they were to continue their friendship after Miranda moves out, and she lets her go without any remorse.

Now living more freely outside her employer's home she slowly develops a relationship with a young man, Peppino. Miranda, whose country upbringing makes it impossible for her to imagine that someone like Peppino could have bad intentions, accepts everything he does as normal and even as signs of love. Their first sexual encounter, described more like a rape than an act of love, seems so violent to Miranda that, as the narrator tells us, "aveva davvero paura di morire" ("she was really afraid she would die") (Viganò 77). When he asks her, mockingly, "Non era mica la prima volta, vero?" ("It wasn't really your first time, right?") she replies, naïvely confused, "Non ho mai fatto l'amore con nessuno" ("I've never made love to anyone"), only to notice that her new silk stockings have been ripped (78).

When Miranda realizes she is pregnant, she seems confident that abortion is not the answer to her problem, but she does not know what her next step should be. She tries to hide her pregnancy, and consoles herself with the "speranza svagata" ("absent-minded hope") that her boss would not fire her when she learns of the pregnancy (131). Ill health gives her away, and one day she faints while she is washing soiled butcher rags. Her brother, Alfio, a young Communist who has also migrated to the city to work, comes to help her. The novel closes with the image of Alfio and Miranda coping with her pregnancy together, her emotional strength regained by the support her brother shows her: "E mentre lei scendeva un po' a fatica, le tocco' appena i capelli, un piccolo gesto timoroso di tenerezza" ("And while she wearily walked down he just barely touched her hair, it was a small gesture, timid and tender") (138). Although Miranda does not know how she will take care of her child and face her parents, she knows that with the help of her brother, everything will work out. Miranda has thus found the solution to her future outside of a conventional romantic heterosexual relationship (even as Alfio becomes a stand-in for the unborn child's father).

At first it seems that the novel calls for a rather conservative position. Viganò, as the authorial voice behind the narrator, seems to argue an antiabortion position, since the protagonist, whom Battistini calls "l'ideale sorella minore di Agnese" ("Agnese's ideal younger sister") does not abort her child, and the young woman who does, Piera, is a bourgeois character.[8] Although Piera, the middle-class woman, has an abortion, something that Miranda, the working-class woman, comes to see as immoral, the novel does more than just espouse an antiabortion position (a position in line with Viganò's own party, the PCI), but rather it rebukes the shame placed on an unwed mother.[9] Viganò turns the shame and guilt women are told to feel into a sense of support and encouragement through the character and rhetoric of Miranda's do-good Communist brother. Explaining to her brother what had happened, Miranda speaks of the shame that had immobilized her for some time: "Mi vergognavo" ("I was ashamed") (138). She then defends herself, her right to love, and her honorable intentions, all the while blaming herself for not recognizing that Peppino did not share her feelings:

Istintivamente difendeva se stessa, l'inizio innocente del suo amore, la pulizia della sua disavventura . . . "E' stata colpa mia. Avrei dovuto capire che non faceva sul serio. Per cento motivi avrei dovuto capire . . . Così stasera"—aggiunse con calma—"volevo darmi la morte." (138)

She instinctively defended herself, the innocence at first of her love, the cleanliness of her misfortune. . . . "It was my fault, I should have understood that he wasn't serious, there were a hundred reasons why I should have understood . . . so tonight"—she added calmly—"I wanted to kill myself."

Thinking along these lines we can see how the novel is more about recognizing women's free will and less about a moralistic stand on abortion. Further, as Codrignani explains, the point of view of the narrative is always a female one, and thus the actual debate on abortion is less important than the acknowledgment of various positions:

Anche se i valori morali sono rappresentati dalla ragazza del popolo che si tiene il figlio e non dalla borghese che abortisce clandestinamente, il tessuto narrativo tesse trame solo femminili. (in E. Colombo, 66)

Even if the moral values are represented by the working-class girl who keeps her child and not by the bourgeois girl who illegally aborts, the narrative fabric weaved is only female.

Similarly, the written narrative brings forth points of view on abortion that were as of then not part of the fabric of middle-class Italian culture. Codrignani reminds us that for 1962, merely discussing such issues was radical and important with respect to the growing women's movement in Italy:

Agli inizi degli anni Sessanta non tutte le donne capivano l'imponenza del problema-aborto: Renata precorre in qualche modo le campagne radicali che le "masse" femminili, operaie e borghesi, laiche e cattoliche percepiranno, in modi diversi, come liberatorie. Il Partito comunista condivideva ancora il moralismo . . . (in E. Colombo 66)

At the beginning of the Sixties, all women did not understand the impressiveness of the abortion problem: Renata somehow anticipates the radical side that the female "masses," workers and the middle class, laywomen and Catholics would perceive, in different ways, as liberatory. The Communist Party still furthered a moralistic view . . .

The PCI supported a conservative position on abortion, which acknowledged the possibility of abortion when the mother's life was in danger, until by much pressure from women's groups, like the *Unione donne italiane* (Udi), the party changed its position in the 1970s.[10] As Bono and Kemp explain, the Udi "influenced many communist women, and it helped them in their effort to bring pressure on the party to modify its policy" (212). Viganò's desire to show a variety of positions on the subject (versus only holding a pro-Communist and an antiabortionist position), is reaffirmed by the novel's representation of PCI members who are not as helpful as Miranda's brother, even under similar circumstances. Mario, Piera's boyfriend, who deserted her when she tells him she is pregnant, is also a Communist. During a conversation between Piera and Miranda that takes place after Piera's abortion, Miranda speaks proudly of her Communist brother, and Piera, bursting her idealistic bubble, points out that not all Communists are so admirable since "è un comunista anche Mario" ("even Mario is a Communist") (83).

In *Una storia di ragazze* we have a simple portrayal of postwar life through the perspective of a strong-willed, though naïve, young woman. Through the fictionalized account of a single domestic worker, Viganò manages to bring to the surface subjects (domestic servitude, abortion, and unwed motherhood) usually left unearthed. Through the failed cross-class alliance between Miranda and Piera, the abortion debate is exposed and brought forward for debate into the public sphere. In so doing, Viganò registers disparate positions, all of which, in the following fifteen years, would become part of the public discussion around the issue of legalizing abortion. By narrating such "private issues"—until then, issues generally excluded from public middle-class discourse—Viganò critically exposes aspects of dominant Italian culture and calls attention to the ways in which social and economic factors—cultural and class differences—all play a part in the formation of a hegemonic culture. That is, by illustrating the complexities of such powerful issues as abortion, Viganò presents the contradictions in thinking in terms of a single worldview or a singular understanding of national identity. Although similar to Gramsci's development of the Marxist Woman Question and his views on the need for recognizing differences among subaltern groups, Viganò moves quite beyond Gramsci with a keen interest in female body politics. The class distinction becomes more pronounced by the heterosexual relationship each young woman has. Thus Viganò in a sense extends the traditional Woman Question by recognizing that class works with and against other normative positions.

Foreign and Domestic

In her *Casalinghe di riserva*, a 1977 sociological study of the state of domestic servants in Italy, Olga Turrini mentions in a footnote the fact that her study did not take into account a recent phenomenon occurring in Italy whereby more and more domestic workers were women of color.[11] While migration within Italy and from Italy toward other countries continued, she notes a shift that seemed to be taking place. To consider this growing occurrence, she explains, would require a study schooled in the nuances of race and ethnicity and the way these categories interact with categories of gender and class, something she is not prepared to do. Her footnote reads as follows:

> Nella nostra ricerca non è stato preso in considerazione un fenomeno che sta assumendo dimensioni sempre più rilevanti: quello delle lavoratrici domestiche di colore. E' un limite del quale siamo ben consapevoli; tuttavia è sembrato preferibile rimandare a un successivo approfondimento l'analisi di un tema che presenta aspetti molto specifici: da quello della provenienza e dei canali di reclutamento a quello dei problemi di inserimento in una società diversa per lingua, cultura, abitudini, a quello del ruolo che si vuole attribuire alle lavoratrici domestiche di colore, di elementi di concorrenza nel mercato del lavoro con le altre domestiche e quindi di ulteriore indebolimento di una categoria che a fatica sta cercando di conquistare migliori condizioni contrattuali. Non sembra dunque corretto affrontare marginalmente e genericamente questi temi che, data anche la difficoltà di definire le dimensioni precise del fenomeno per mancanza di dati, richiederebbero una specifica indagine "ad hoc." (34)

> In our research we did not take into consideration a phenomenon which is always assuming more relevant dimensions: that of the female domestic worker of color. It is a limitation of which we are very conscious; nevertheless, it seems preferable to leave this analysis for a future careful investigation because it is a subject which has many specific aspects: from the channels of recruitment for workers to that of the problem of assimilation in a society that differs linguistically, culturally, and in habit; from the role that we want to give to women domestic workers of color to the element of competition in the labor market with other women domestic workers and therefore the further weakening of a category [of labor] which, with much difficulty, is trying to gain better contractual agreements. It does not, therefore, seem right to confront marginally and generically these subjects which, given the difficulty in trying to define the precise dimension of the phenomenon because of a lack of data, would require a more specific "ad hoc" research.

Although Turrini should be commended for her foresight and her recognition of the multifacetedness of the situation, today the high numbers of foreign-born domestic workers in Italy make it imperative that we go beyond a footnote in examining the situation. Today the question of migration in Italy has an added complexity: the fact that the majority of migration occurs from extra-Italian locations, locations as geopolitically disparate as Ghana, the Ukraine, and Bolivia.[12] Domestic labor remains one of the few types of employment open to women immigrants (documented and undocumented)—while more and more male immigrants are also working as domestics, my focus here remains on the labor of women.[13] Once again we have a circumstance where the lives of women laborers are marginalized and isolated. The difference now is that this exclusion involves very distinct racial, cultural, and national boundaries.

Contemporary publications by and about immigrants to Italy include testimonials, novels, poetry, and drama. Since the late 1980s Italian immigrants have made their voices heard by native Italians through authoring various cultural texts in Italian. The majority of these texts are authored by men, and only a handful or so have female authors.[14] The experiences of domestic workers are generally left out or marginalized within most of these narratives. Instead, they are brought to the attention of the Italian reader via a variety of collections of interviews, testimonials, and oral stories. Many examples of such storytelling exist in the pages of conference proceedings, photocopied pamphlets, and newspaper articles.[15] Others, however, have found their way to texts published by large, national publishing houses and are financially backed by a variety of government, business, and university monies.[16] The fact that we must look to unconventional forms of narrative in order to discuss the representation of contemporary domestic workers confirms the continued marginal status women and women's labor is afforded in dominant Italian culture and reinforces the necessity of such interventions as this one. It also suggests the importance of different kinds of knowledge (akin to Gramsci's common sense and good sense) that can lead (in sometimes contradictory ways) to a counter-hegemony.

Moreover, the form of documentation of the women's lives available to us—mediated, first-person accounts or testimonials—functions as a reminder of the contradictory space women hold within Italy. As Lisa Lowe notes with respect to testimonials by Asian American women: "To consider testimony and testimonial as constituting a 'genre' of cultural production is significant for Asian immigrant women, for it extends the scope of what constitutes legitimate knowledges to include other forms and practices that have been traditionally excluded from both empirical and aesthetic modes of evaluation"

(156). Recognizing these narratives as texts open to interpretation and analysis allows for an understanding of the women's positions with respect to an Italian national popular culture and the potentiality of an alternative international popular culture.

The two 1990s' collections of immigrant women's autobiographical narratives discussed here—Giuliano Carlini's *La terra in faccia* and Amelia Crisantino's *Ho trovato l'occidente*—differ somewhat in structure. Carlini's *La terra in faccia* (*Dirt in the Face*) has sixteen discrete (two- to three-page-long) transcribed first-person testimonials by immigrant men and women (eight of each) and separate critical essays written by the interviewers and researchers. On the other hand, Amelia Crisantino's *Ho trovato l'occidente* (*I've Discovered the West*) intertwines Cristantino's first-person account about meeting various immigrant women with the women's own stories, stories that are placed in quotations in order to emphasize the fact that the words are not Crisantino's.[17] What the two collections share structurally is that both give only the first name (or no name) of most of the immigrants and that the immigrants' grammar has been altered to reflect standard Italian. In short, each collection is the result of numerous editorial choices that affect the way the narratives are received by their readers.[18]

Reviewing these autobiographical narratives offers an understanding of how the women's lives and their stories help constitute a distinct hegemonic cultural identity. Furthermore, these narratives show how the women at times distance themselves from those identities and also feel excluded from them by others. While each woman's relationship to and experiences with Italy differs, none of them defines herself as Italian. Even those women who have lived in Italy for many years, hold legal residency (there is no information given about citizenship), and have a pension do not think of themselves as Italian. They (and the interviewers) continue to create an us/them dichotomy, refusing to recognize their own contribution to Italian culture, or to see themselves as Italian. Nonetheless the women, in their descriptions of life in Italy, seem to know what it means to be Italian. That is, Italian culture is self-evident to them in that they articulate their situation outside of that identity. Thus these narratives (and the labor they describe) construct an understanding of middle-class Italian identity that for the most part excludes and isolates immigrants.

In discussing the immigrant situation today in Italy it is sometimes difficult to know exactly how general or specific one should be. Even though the focus here is on immigrant women domestic workers, such specificity still leaves us with women from numerous countries of origin.[19] Because they come from such different locations, it is easy to forget their histories and focus only on what they have in common—their position as foreign-born female domestic workers who live and work in Italy.[20] Yet, the women, even though (or precisely because) their stories are mediated through editors, remind us constantly of their uniqueness. In fact, while many collections of testimonials create apparent alliances between women, the women themselves rarely express any sense of intergroup solidarity. In Teresa Picarazzi's discussion of a similar collection, she argues that the repeated autobiographical effect of having first-person narratives "refutes/challenges our tendency to generalize over the plight of the migrant woman" (305). In fact, in both collections, the women's insistence on sharing their stories of what brought them to Italy suggests that they sense how easy it would be to overlook their differences.

In addition to describing in detail their life histories—their lives in their native countries and what brought them to Italy—the women discuss their association with native Italians and Italy generally. All in all, the women describe a precarious relationship to Italian culture (a culture that for them is generally unified and undifferentiated). While on occasion a woman explains that she married an Italian or has very close Italian friends, most of the women describe one-sided or nonexistent relationships with Italians. They feel like strangers in a strange land and describe a life outside of the middle-class Italian life of most of their employers. One Eritrean woman who has been in Italy working as a domestic servant since 1964 explains that while the life of an immigrant has become much easier over the last thirty years, some things have not changed: "Anche ora non abbiamo amici italiani . . . stiamo sempre tra di noi" ("Even now we don't have Italian friends . . . we always stay with each other") (in Crisantino 26). Similarly, in *La terra in faccia*, a Bolivian woman explains: "Ho visto che qui tanti italiani, donne o uomini che siano, hanno paura di parlare con uno straniero" ("I have seen here that many Italians, women and men the same, are afraid to talk to strangers/foreigner") (in Carlini 115). Generally, the women do not link this feeling of estrangement to a sense of racial or ethnic prejudice but only to their position as foreigners or outsiders.

While the collection documents some moments of racism, the majority of the immigrants do not connect their feelings of estrangement to their racial or ethnic status; but what they do emphasize is that to be Italian means not being a domestic worker. One woman from Cape Verde explains that "In Italia c'è tanta gente, peró è diverso, la gente ti vede sempre straniera" ("There are a lot of people in Italy, but it's different, people always see you as a stranger") (in Carlini 43). She goes on to tell a story about one time at the grocery store when she pointed out to the cashier that she had been given the wrong amount of change. While the cashier was straightening out the

Migrant Domestic Labor and the Creation of Identity 71

transaction, a man behind her in line, asked "Chi vi ha mandato qua?" ("Who sent you here?") (43). Such situations, she claims, "ti rimangono sempre dentro" ("always remain inside you"). But she concludes that it is common between people who do not know each other, and she does not connect it to racial discrimination: "Communque succede sempre con le persone che non ti conoscono" ("However, it happens often with people who don't know you") (43). This alienation comes not only from Italians; that is, many women acknowledge little or no connection to immigrants from other countries—there are no cross-immigrant alliances. One of Crisantino's many "guides" through immigrant communities in Palermo, Tina, from Madagascar, states this type of isolation point blank:

> E' molto difficile che si diventi amiche fra diverse ethnie. Per i bianchi queste donne sono tutte uguali, ma fra di noi ci sono le stesse differencee che fra uno svizzero e un siciliano. Sono quelli della Costa d'Avorio e forse i ghanesi ad essere più disponibili, andrebbero volentieri con gli altri gruppi. Ma nessuno li vuole. Le donne che sono qua da più tempo, come le filippine, e le capoverdiane, formano dei gruppi chiusi. (122)

> It is very difficult to form friendships between different ethnic women. For whites these women are all the same, but for us the same differences exist as between a Swiss and a Sicilian. Immigrants from the Ivory Coast, and perhaps from Ghana, are more open, and would gladly go out with people in other groups. But no one wants them. Women who have been here for some time, like the Filipinas and the Capeverdians, form closed groups.

This seemingly self-imposed ethnic ghettoization also surfaces in the form of a lack of understanding between immigrant women from different places. Alfonsine, a Mauritius woman, explains the way the migrant is racialized differently by Italians and by immigrants, like herself:

> A Palermo le donne più richeste sono le mauriziane e le filippine, stanno anche vent'anni nella stessa famiglia. . . . Quelle che non vuole nessuno sono le donne che vengono dal Ghana, dalla Costa d'Avorio. Sono nere nere, strane. Sono sempre puzzolenti, anche se si lavano c'è sempre questo odore di selvaggio, da quelle parti sono selvaggi . . . Quelle nere fanno impressione, e poi loro sono di carattere, le mauriziane e le filippine sono più calme. Noi non discutiamo. Diciamo: "va bene." E poi quelle nere non vogliono restare a dormire, vogliono essere più libere. (Crisantino 50–51)

> In Palermo women from Mauritius and the Philippines are the most sought after, sometimes they even stay in the same family for twenty years. . . . Those

women whom no one wants are from Ghana and from the Ivory Coast. They are black, black, strange. They always smell, even when they wash themselves they always have this savage smell about them, in those parts the people are savage. . . . The black women make people feel uncomfortable, and then they are of a certain character, Mauritius and Filipina women are calmer. We don't argue. We say: "Okay." And then the black women don't want to live at their workplaces, they want to have more freedom.

Alfonsine describes a situation whereby the racist discourse of the dominant culture gets rearticulated and confirmed by minority classes—pitting immigrant against immigrant.

Alfonsine's characterization of immigrant relationships is unique, for when racist sentiments are raised by women, they are usually describing racism against them by native Italians. Crisantino, for example, tells the story of Marlene, a thirty-seven-year-old woman from Mauritius. She married a Sicilian man whom she met ten years ago, and she continues to work as a domestic. She asserts there is little racism: "Qualche volta è capitato che hanno parlato contro di me, per la strada. Io penso: non m'interssa, la mia pelle è così, non m'interessa quello che dicono, e quasi non li sento" ("Sometimes it's happened that someone has said something against me on the street. I think: I don't care, my skin is this color, and I don't care what that person says, and I almost don't hear them") (46). Other women also articulate a sense of racism that they experience not within the home of their employers but on the streets, by strangers. One Eritrean woman who has been in Italy for eighteen years claims that she has never experienced racism, though, lately, she had felt that she was different:

> Io non ho mai conosciuto che cosa sia il razzismo. . . . anche quando sono venuta in Italia, io non ho sentito di essere differente. Ora, in questi due o tre anni, sento di essere diversa, non che io l'abbia voluto, ma ci fanno sentire. Ecco, questo è il problema. Anche se non riesco a capirlo, però mi fanno sentire lo stesso così: lo vedo, in autobus, per la strada, o anche nei mezzi di informazione. (61)

> I have never known racism. . . . even when I came to Italy, I never felt like I was different. Now, in the last two or three years, I feel like I am different, not that I wanted to feel this way, but they make me feel it. Look, this is the problem. Even if I don't understand it, but they nonetheless make me feel like this: I see it on the bus, on the street, or even in the media.

Still other women recognize the existence of racism by noting their (unintentional) capacity to mask their immigrant status, and thus mask their racial status. When Crisantino asks Fatima, a woman from Tunisia who lives in Sicily, if she had ever encountered racism, Fatima answers: "Io no, mi scambiano tutti per siciliana. Ma non sono una siciliana, e non voglio diventarci. Sono orgogliosa di essere araba" ("Me, no, they think I'm Sicilian. But I'm not Sicilian, and I don't want to be. I'm proud to be Arab") (in Crisantino 103). Such a comment, of course, implies that racism does exist, because Fatima's experience is related to the way she looks. In much the same way, a woman from Peru also suggests that the reaction an immigrant gets from Italians has to do with the way he or she is racialized by Italians: "Con la gente italiana—non so se a me ha aiutato la pelle che non è troppo scura, ho un po' di indio, ma . . . —mi sono trovata sempre bene" (" I've always gotten along well with Italians—I don't know if maybe it helped that I'm not very dark, I have some Indian in me, but . . . [in Carlini 71]).

In all of these examples of different experiences in Italy what is most peculiar is that the women always portray themselves as outside of Italian culture and outside of any definition of "being Italian." Even those women who explain that they never experience racism because of their skin color never go on to say that they, therefore, feel close to Italians. Fatima, for one, reasserts her foreignness, stating forcefully that she does not want to be Italian (in Crisantino 103). Thus in these narratives we find women who distance themselves (and are distanced by others) from Italian culture. Their insistence on recognizing their position as outsiders acts as a strategic declaration of their own national/racial/cultural identity. Moreover, by negating their position as Italians, the women outline what it means to be Italian. That is, one outcome of underscoring their differences and the lack of strong bonds with native Italians is that the women paint a picture of what it means to be Italian and live in Italy in the late twentieth century. For the women, having an Italian identity, first of all, means not working as a domestic worker—a point that almost erases de facto the story (past or present) of Italian-born domestic workers. When the contradictions and differences between each woman are taken into consideration, their stories share a narrative point of view as foreign-born domestic workers.

Far from creating a national popular culture that represents their experiences, they in fact seem almost to further support one that excludes them. Moreover, that the women do not support alliances across national boundaries is a token of their exclusion. In theory, once their identity is firmly established, they might be able to form such international alliances, ones that would lead to the development of an international popular culture. In effect, by talking to Italians in the form of these testimonials, a foundation is laid. The testimonials themselves form the basis of a new international popular culture by demonstrating a complex idea of cultural identity—one that the women arrive at in part by coming into contact with others.

The women's comments on their jobs help secure a hegemonic positionality for native Italians and simultaneously situate the women outside of that position. A woman from the Philippines who was an elementary school teacher back home and has lived and worked as a domestic in Italy for almost two decades considers the low value given to her labor:

> Certi ci guardano male perché siamo domestici, però è un lavoro pulito, non c'è da vergognarsi e si guadagna bene. A me non importa molto se la gente mi tratta così, perché adesso so parlare e so combattere, ma di solito incontro gente bene. (in Carlini 65)
>
> Certain people look on us badly because we are domestics, but it is a clean job, there's no reason to be ashamed and we get paid well. I don't care much if people treat me like that, because now I know how to speak [Italian] and I know how to fight, but usually I meet good people.

This woman's reasoning demonstrates one way in which domestic workers are made to feel outside of certain prescribed notions of everyday culture in Italy. If her labor is degraded by others, then it makes sense that she would not see herself (or be seen by others) as part of general society.

The sense of isolation many immigrant women describe, an isolation that keeps them detached from the everyday practices of their Italian native-born neighbors, is related to the domestic workers' slippery position between private and public spaces. In particular, domestic workers who live at their place of employment must balance a constant outsidedness while they are inside the home. Regardless of where they live, when they are out on the street they are often marked as an other—as one woman from Peru explains:

> C'è da dire che il disagio che si prova a essere fisso è questo; tante volte uno preferirebbe rimanere a casa a riposarsi, ma c'è da decidere: mi riposo e non vedo gli amici, non mi distraggo, anche mentalmente—perché, oltre alla stanchezza fisica, a stare sempre dentro, ci si stanca anche mentalmente. . . ; ma anche stando fuori ci stancavamo e non avevamo neanche dove andare, qualche volta ci toccava andare al cinema e qualcuno dormiva invece di guardare il film, o andavamo a messa. (in Carlini 72–73)
>
> I should add that the disadvantage of living at one's employers is this: many times one would prefer to stay at home to relax, but instead one has to make a decision: should I stay at home and not see my friends, I won't distract myself,

not even mentally—because, on top of being physically tired, one gets tired mentally, just from being inside all the time. . . ; but also staying outside is tiring and we didn't always have a place to go, sometimes we had to go to the movies and someone always fell asleep instead of watching the film, or we would go to mass.

She can never be at home where she lives, because her work is all around her, and since her chance of forming a friendship with someone in the home is quite minimal, public city spaces remain the only locations open to her for forming intimate friendships. Having no space within the location where she works or lives to call her own, the female immigrant domestic worker (a commodity both inside and outside the home) becomes the human embodiment of the global market—the transnational movement of goods and people. When that woman is also racialized by the people around her, this representation is made stronger. Thus the female immigrant domestic worker, whether at home or in a public space, contributes to the construction of an Italian national popular culture as she is simultaneously excluded from it. This exclusion in turn solidifies her own identity as a member of a marginalized group. From this dual recognition of difference the potential for future alliances is paradoxically founded.

While there are no glaring examples of racism, discrimination, or prejudice against immigrants within their places of employment, we must assume that such discrimination does in fact exist. Even if the women discuss racism only in terms of people who do not know them on the street (a function perhaps of certain constraints of the interview/oral narrative structure), a kind of structural racism exists, suggested by the mere fact that practically the only job open to immigrant women is domestic work. The women are obliged to work as domestics because of their birthplace, not because they are not qualified to do something else. Obvious markers of their foreignness, such as language barriers, deflect into class barriers between immigrants and native Italians, making friendships or alliances almost impossible. Unlike the internal migration and emigration of Italian natives, this new wave of immigration is made up of high numbers of well-educated adults, who are leaving their native countries because of political turmoil coupled with unstable economies. It is not unlikely for a domestic servant from the Philippines to be a school teacher, a maid from Ghana a doctor, and a servant from Croatia a lawyer—Palazzi explains:

> Per le lavoratrici immigrate l'assorbimento in questa occupazione non è legato in generale, come avveniva precedentemente per le italiane, alle condizioni di

istruzione, cultura, competenze professionali. Ci sono donne diplomate, donne che nel loro paese hanno acquistato professionalità specifica . . . (22–23)

For immigrant women workers the absorption into this occupation is not tied, like it was in the past for Italian women, to conditions of education, culture, or professional competence. There are women with high school degrees, women who in their countries have achieved a certain professional status . . .

Related is the fact that the arrival of more and more immigrant women who "willingly" take (often low-paying) jobs as domestic workers coincided (not coincidentally) with middle-class, Italian-born women's escape from oppressive family conditions at home and entrance (in no small numbers) into professional careers. As Palazzi states candidly: The rise in immigrant women who take jobs as domestic workers "ha avuto il processo di emancipazione delle donne Italiane" ("managed to emancipate Italian women") (23). Keeping these issues in mind, it is impossible to dismiss the structural racism that exists in Italy.

One possible reason for this structural racism is that these women's relationship to any sense of a privileged Italian culture is precarious. Perhaps, though, this relationship will change over time as the European Union expands. As more and more movement between national boundaries occurs and as the children of Italian immigrants grow up, perhaps the women and their families will more visibly affect Italian culture in such a way as to make their contribution and existence recognizable by all. The mere existence of these oral story collections and other novels by immigrants are signs of such cultural transformations, signs of the potentiality for an international popular culture. We can imagine how the women's diverse histories and experiences coupled with their role as domestic workers—a labor that by definition helps create and sustain the culture of everyday life—might point to the transformative potential the women have on their work and living environments.

Notes

1. She argues for a materialist-based "libertà *nel* lavoro, non *dal* lavoro" ("liberty *in* work, not *from* it") (115; emphasis in original). In typical Diotima fashion, she intertwines Marxist theory, a feminist theory of social-symbolic practice, and an acknowledgment of her own privileged status as a philosophy professor.
2. See Hazel Carby or Linda Kerber.
3. Such scholarship is in line with feminist critiques of labor histories (discussed in the introduction), which show the ways in which gender and racial identities have been excluded from much of the historical studies of labor.

4. Even though both meat dishes take a few hours to cook, the housewife version is more labor intensive. The major difference in the two meat dishes is that the domestic servant version is basically a two-step process (cut up all ingredients and cook), whereas the housewife version has an additional initial step, common to Italian cooking, the *soffritto*, the mixture of *aromi* (usually onions or garlic with various herbs) sautéed together with something like olive oil or a little piece of pork fat before the other ingredients of the dish are added. This dish also has an additional final step—straining the meat juices and pouring them over the roast.

5. Battistini explains that Viganò was committed to being a "portavoce delle aberrazini della società, di denunciare i soprusi subiti dai più deboli, di rendersi insomma utile ai lettori, stabilendo con loro un contatto diretto e umano. E la solidarietà si esercita sopratutto verso le donne . . ." ("spokesperson for the aberrations in society, to denounce those who take advantage of the weakest people, that is, to make herself useful to her readers, establishing a direct and human contact with them. And, above all, this solidarity is exercised toward women" (in Colombo, *Matrimonio in brigata* 43).

6. See *Noi Donne*, Anno VIII, n. 24, June 14, 1953, 2. Viganò wrote advice columns for both *Noi Donne* and *Il Progresso d'Italia*. See Giancarla Codrignani (in Colombo, *Matrimonio in brigata*) for a brief review of her advice letters. Other *Noi Donne* columnists also wrote about domestic workers. See, for instance, Anno VIII, n. 37, 6–7, September 20, 1959, for a short story by Aldo Scagnetti, "La domestica, un cuore solidario." Viganò also wrote a short story, "Mai da loro" (unpublished manuscript, [1959]) about a female domestic worker who withstands her boss's harassment since he has promised to give her husband a job (ANPI archive, Bologna, "Racconti 1–34").

7. Next to no scholarship has been written on this novel. Viganò's second novel, *L'Agnese va a morire*, remains canonized in the Italian literary tradition, yet her complete oeuvre is mostly out of print and rarely read today or engaged with critically. This section refers to two articles, both of which briefly discuss *Una storia di ragazze*. Both pieces (by Battistini and Codrignani) were published in the museum catalogue of a show in Bologna about her and her husband, Antonio Meluschi. (See chapter one for further discussion of Viganò.)

8. Battistini refers to Viganò's most famous character, Agnese, the partisan washerwoman in *L'Agnese va a morire*.

9. Nine years earlier in *Noi Donne*, Viganò explained her position on single motherhood, a position that comes to bear directly on her characters in *Una storia di ragazze*. Responding to a young, pregnant, unmarried woman, Viganò writes:

> Essere madre e non sposa, avere la propria creatura tra le braccia e trovarsi sola a farla crescere non deve essere per te motivo di vergogna. Deve, se mai, vergognarsi l'uomo che non ha fatto fronte al suo dovere ed ha lasciato nel mondo un figlio senza protezione. (Anno VIII, n. 39, October 4, 1953, 2)

> To be a mother and not a wife, to have one's own child in one's arms and find oneself raising him alone should not be a reason for you to feel ashamed. If anything, the man who

did not face his responsibility and who left his son alone and unprotected in the world, he's the one who should be ashamed.

10. The Udi was founded in September 1944. It was originally made up of women from all parts of Italy who were united against Fascism, but it quickly became associated with Communism. Lucia Chiavola Birnbaum in her *liberazione delle donne* explains that while many Catholic women belonged to the Udi, they later joined the Christian Democratic Party (DC), and formed the Centro Italiano femminile; both groups, however, came together to fight for the vote, which women obtained in January 1945. By the late 1940s, Udi was and would continue to be an unofficial extension of the Italian Communist Party (PCI) and related successor parties. The Udi publishes the magazine *noidonne* (which has evolved from *Noi Donne*, to *noi donne* after 1968, to *noidonne* in 1982 and noidonne.org in 2005). For a succinct history of Udi and *noidonne* see Birnbaum.

11. While Turrini does not specify, she is referring to the increasing numbers of men and women migrating to Italy from countries in North Africa and Southeast Asia. Today large numbers of immigrants also come to Italy from the former Eastern Bloc, the Middle East, and South America.

12. The Italian government calls these immigrants *extracomunitari* referring to the *comunità*, the community of Europe. See the introduction for more information on the countries of origin.

13. Italian internal migration, especially emigration from Sardegna, Sicily, and southern regions to northern regions, claims its own set of very real racial, ethnic, and cultural concerns. Beyond the scope of this chapter is a discussion of the past and continued north/south disparity sustained by conservative politicians and cultural critics. This long-standing disparity, often supported by a racialization of southerners as nonwhite, was strengthened by the colonization of the south during the Risorgimento. The success of a political party such as Umberto Bossi's Lega Lombarda is proof enough of the continued north/south divide. Moreover, Bossi's anti-south and anti-immigrant position is suggested by the way he links southerners and immigrants through discursively reasserting long-standing, pejorative claims about southerners as "half Africans," and pitting immigrants against Italy's southerners when discussing unemployment. Italy's newest residents, though, are part of a different racial presence, related to the old one, but nonetheless deserving of special consideration. See Donald Clark (esp. chapter eight), David Ward (in Allen and Russo), and Verdicchio (*Bound by Distance*) for critical interventions on these issues.

14. At least two novels have been authored by women immigrants: Nassera Chohra's *Volevo diventare bianca* and Maria Viarengo's *Andiamo a spasso*. Both of these novels narrate the lives of women with a high degree of economic privilege and do not, for the most part, consider issues of labor pertinent to my discussion. Graziella Parati, in one of the few academic studies of these books, argues that Viarengo and Chohra come from a position of economic privilege, so that their experiences as immigrant women cannot be held as an example of most women migrating to Italy. See

also Amara Lakhous's mystery novel, *Scontro di civiltà per un ascensore a piazza Vittorio*, for a main character who is a domestic worker. On Italian immigrant narratives and culture generally see Biasin, Clò and Fiore, Fiore Gnisci, Parati, Picarazzi, Ruberto, and Verdicchio, and Zinn.

15. See, for instance, the proceedings from the conference in Modena, Italy, on October 28, 1995, called, "La condizione della donna e della bambina africana," sponsored by various city health services and the Udi; or the conference proceedings of Emilia-Romagna's regional conference, "L'Emigrazione al femminile," held on January 12–13, 1990 (mentioned at the beginning of this chapter).

16. For instance, *La terra in faccia: Gli immigrati raccontano*, edited by Giuliano Carlini (1991), was a collaborative research project funded by the Ires Liguria (Institute of Economic and Social Research) requested by Cgil (Italian General Confederation of Labor) and the Camera del Lavoro di Genova (Local Units of the Cgil) with the aid of the Political Science Institute of the University of Genova. On the other hand, Amelia Crisantino's short interviews with immigrant women in her *Ho trovato l'occidente: Storie di donne immigrate a Palermo* (1992) are related to her profession as a sociologist, but the book was not visibly sponsored by a government or institution.

17. Laura Gambi, a social worker in Ravenna, has published a narrative that is similar to Crisantino's. In Teresa Picarazzi's examination of Gambi's text, Picarazzi notes Gambi's self-conscious reflection on her privileged role as interviewer, transcriber, and editor; Picarazzi concludes, "however absent she is in the narratives of the other women. . . . Gambi is, nonetheless the medium through which we have access to these women" (307).

18. Borrowing from Chandra Talpede Mohanty, Lowe also reminds us that "the way we read, receive, and disseminate" such narratives is as important of a step as recording the narratives in the first place (Lowe 66). See my "Immigrants Speak" for a critical discussion of these particular texts' production and reception in Italy.

19. The women and men interviewed in these collections come from the following countries (in alphabetical order): Brazil, Bolivia, Cape Verde, Eritrea, Ghana, Iran, India, Madagascar, Mauritius, Morocco, Nigeria, Peru, the Philippines, Seychelles, Sri Lanka, and Tunisia.

20. Lowe theorizes the terms hybridity, heterogeneity, and multiplicity in order to name "the material contradictions that characterize Asian American groups" (67). Reading Asian American culture through an articulation of these terms allows for a recognition of varied histories and experiences, challenges traditional notions about aesthetics, and offers alternative notions of "dominant" and "minority" discourse. Perhaps these Italian immigrant books could be read with a similar process. See, in particular, Lowe, chapter three.

CHAPTER THREE

Work and the Italian American Home in Cinema

> Frank Costello eating spaghetti in a cell at San Quentin
> Lucky Luciano mixing up a mess of bullets and calling for parmesan cheese,
> Al Capone baking a sawed-off shotgun into a huge lasagna—
> are you my uncles, my only uncles?
>
> —Sandra M. Gilbert, "Mafioso"

When Henry Hill, in Martin Scorsese's *Goodfellas*, describes in his voiceover narration the multicourse meals he and his buddies prepared for themselves while in prison, he is participating in a long-standing cinematic tradition. As an Italian American gangster, part of his screen presence and his personality is articulated through explicit and repeated connections to food and its preparation.[1] As the epigraph shows, literary critic, creative writer, and "cryptoethnic" Sandra Mortola Gilbert uses a similar relationship of food to mafiosi to question popular images of Italians in the United States.[2] In her poem "Mafioso," she directly links the mobster profession with the art of cooking and asks if these two kinds of labor are the only way in which Italian American men can be remembered or understood. In the following pages, the idea of gangsters as cooks leads into a discussion of cinematic representations of Italian American kitchens and the relationship between everyday, unpaid, domestic labor, Italian American assimilation, and the representation of culture. Gramsci's theories about the creation of national popular culture, especially in relation to folklore and organic intellectuals, directs my discussion and makes apparent the need for a complex analysis of the constitution of ethnic identity within the changing landscape of the United States, especially in relation to consumer culture, assimilation, and gender roles.

The gangster-as-cook image aids in creating the idea of a complex criminal.[3] The wiseguy facing the stove suggests a domestic family man, and the image literally feeds the notion of the Italian mobster's uniqueness within the world of criminals. The godfather who can fix a home-cooked meal for twenty has a certain passion and sensitivity lacking from most nonethnic white criminals. The use of this motif becomes even more interesting when we stop to question the relationship Italian American women have to domestic labors such as cooking. The image of Italian American women in the kitchen remains a mainstay of U.S. popular culture; however, the gangster film—arguably the most popular form of Italian American culture—oddly enough breaks that cliché. In mobster films, the labor of women, in particular that performed within the home, is decidedly absent. This absence sustains a kind of "rhetoric of nostalgia" (a term borrowed from anthropologist Micaela di Leonardo) that ignores historical realities about Italians in the United States and distorts the discourse about Italians' assimilation in U.S. culture generally.[4]

Here the rhetoric of nostalgia figures prominently, particularly as it relates to U.S. cinema. More specifically, I examine the domestic space of the kitchen and the daily, unwaged labor performed within it, in order to explore the connection between cinematic images of Italian American women and the discursive production of Italian American culture. By reviewing specific mainstream cinematic versions of the Italian American experience (through short readings of Martin Scorsese's *Goodfellas* and Francis Ford Coppola's *The Godfather*), I explore how Italian American assimilation into middle-class America is integrally linked to a privileging of a white, middle-class narrative, a narrative that requires that the waged and unwaged labor of Italian American women be overlooked. Further, through a close analysis of two films, Nancy Savoca's *Household Saints* and Helen de Michiel's *Tarantella*, I study how unpaid housework performed by Italian American women functions as at once a complex, defining image and a recurring stereotype. These films comment on and construct a vision of the past that recognizes the labor of women, calls attention to the false split between public and private spheres, and documents ways in which Italian Americans have changed over generations. These two cinematic narratives document the inconsistencies, paradoxes, and contradictions of Italian immigrant life. Both films create stories that reflect multiple layers of identities for Italian American women and evoke Gramsci in their emphasis on the culture of everyday life, the strategic use of folk culture (related to his idea of "common sense"), and on a kind of female organic intellectual. Savoca and de Michiel create images of Italian Americans' pasts that refuse to romanticize and at the same time construct what Teresa de Lauretis might call real "historical beings" (10). In a sense, we can think of their work as similar to that of Italian American women writers. As Mary Jo Bona explains in introducing her edited collection of Italian American women writers (*The Voices We Carry*), these writers

> reconstruct the lives of their parents and grandparents in order to celebrate their ancestors success and to negotiate their own positions as second and third generation Italian/American writers. . . . They value the strength of their grandmothers and mothers, they steer away from romanticizing the figure of the mother as perpetually dolorous, essentially good and/or always responsible and attentive. (14)

In *Tarantella* and *Household Saints* the gendered labor of housework is foregrounded, and emphasis is placed on documenting the creation of Italian American culture through everyday domestic work, spirituality, and memory. Directors like Savoca and de Michiel create unsentimental images of Italian American assimilation experiences, and therefore more completely acknowledge the movement of Italian Americans into a white middle-class position. In so doing, Savoca and de Michiel participate in the kind of reimagining of culture that is akin to Gramsci's theories, one that strives in this case to create a national popular culture based on the everyday experiences of women.

Cinema and the Rhetoric of Nostalgia

Recognizing the different ways in which the history of Italian American women has been represented can help deconstruct dominant narratives about the history of Italians in the United States, specifically as those narratives relate to assimilation and generational changes. In *Ready-to-Wear and Ready-to-Work*, a study of immigrant garment women workers in Paris and New York City, Nancy L. Green similarly suggests that examining immigrant women's roles could perhaps create a sustainable dialogue about culture generally:

> Just as earlier analyses of women's work have emphasized gender over class or ethnicity, ethnic studies have generally overlooked women in two important ways. On the one hand, the immigrant worker has been largely conceptualized as a young, single male. On the other, ethnic business theorists have been writing more about capital than about labor, more about entrepreneurs than their

workers, and, implicitly if not explicitly, more about men than about women. A growing body of literature has begun to put gender back into immigrant studies and ethnicity into gender studies. Can "immigrant women" bridge the epistemological gap between two discrete categories of analysis? (172)

A growing number of labor histories intervene on the lack of historical information about Italian immigrant women's labor contributions.[5] This invisibility has a cinematic articulation. That is, the historical absence helps perpetuate a myth visualized on screen that Italian American women did not work at all, a myth that produces a false nostalgia for a past that never existed. If, for example, we focus on the largest wave of Italian emigration (at the beginning of the nineteenth century), we discover that in addition to the responsibility of running their households, women were often employed in canneries or sweatshops or did piecework at home. Jerre Mangione and Ben Morreale, while only allotting a few pages to women's lives in their 500-page-tome, *La Storia: Five Centuries of the Italian American Experience*, identify the complexity of women's experiences. They recognize that turn-of-the-century women worked for wages and contributed to their families and communities, all the while restricted by a lack of education and domineering fathers and husbands (335). Mangione and Morreale also comment on how films and television have created and sustained the stereotype of "the Italian American wife who suffers her lot in silence, only shouting 'Mangia, Mangia!' from time to time" (335). This stereotype has both caused and been affected by a rhetorical paradigm that ignores the complexities of Italian American women's histories, a paradigm that Micaela di Leonardo in an ethnographic study of Italian Americans in California calls a rhetoric of nostalgia. This discursive nostalgia remains the norm within Hollywood films that feature Italian American themes or stories, and it is in part what filmmakers, such as Savoca and de Michiel, work against in their films.

Whatever their commitment to invoking reality, textual representations (historical, creative, or other) remain only representations. Thus, as Robert Stam reminds us, film remains "a mediated version of an already textualized and discursivised socio-ideological world" (in Freidman 252). Through this recognition of a complex textuality we can negotiate the relationship between filmic image and historical reality. Stam creates a methodology for reading "ethnic American" films by cinematically interpreting Mikhail Bakhtin's theories of discourse, utterance, and voice. In cinema (as elsewhere), Stam argues, "complete realism is an impossibility," yet "spectators themselves come equipped with a 'sense of the real' rooted in their own social experience, on the basis of which they can accept, question, or even subvert a film's representations" (254). In these terms, the rhetoric of nostalgia becomes a product of the collaboration between an uninformed viewer and a film that deals in stereotypes. Stam's "sense of the real"—which we might think of as akin to Gramsci's "common sense"—suggests a way in which an audience can resist the ahistorical and clichéd representations common to Hollywood cinema.[6]

The rhetoric of nostalgia when superimposed on films by and about Italian Americans contributes to the fact that most such films portray women outside of labor (waged and unwaged). Such representations suggest that Italian American women never worked, a rhetorical strategy that creates a false nostalgia for a past that never existed. This false nostalgia is a component of the hegemonic discourse that creates and sustains a particular image of Italian American culture and experience. In the introduction to her historical study of Italian American women in New York City, *Workshop to Office*, Miriam Cohen discusses the complicated relationship between Italian Americans and patriarchal culture in order to show that Italian American women took an active role in their communities. She explains that both:

> in Italy and the United States women acted in seemingly contradictory ways that cannot be summarized simply as outgrowths of patriarchal norms. Patriarchal ideals were strained, indeed, violated, as people struggled to meet the realities of everyday life. Within the family arena, the women never had been deferential and passive; they made important decisions about family members. (7)

Cohen, who also invokes di Leonardo, explains inconsistencies between popular culture and stereotypes about Italian Americans versus what a nuanced study of history and women's roles in society tells us:

> It is particularly difficult to shed the stereotype of Italian women because descendants identify ethnicity with an idealized past in which women stayed home and served the men. But the rhetorical nostalgia is just that—a romanticized image of the past, invoked most often (but not exclusively) by men, that denies the real context of ancestors' lives. In neither Southern Italy nor in New York did Italian women live sheltered lives or remain in the shadow of their male kin. In both countries Italian women were called upon to work outside the home, and they were ready when needed to defend the family's interest in the marketplace and with law enforcement officers, school personnel, and representatives of welfare agencies. (7)

The idea of a past steeped in some kind of distorted collective memory—that of an imagined community *a la* Benedict Anderson—illustrates why an examination of cinematic representations of Italian American identity is crucial to an exploration of how the image of Italian American women at work has been transmitted culturally and collectively. Film, by definition a mediated representation, provides a unique opportunity for decoding images that on various levels are related to "real life" and in turn affect the recording and memory of history. Gramsci's insistence on a national popular culture based on the lives of the subaltern classes suggests the need for strategies that can recognize when culture is pressed into the service of the nation-state and thus fails to legitimate the experiences of subalterns.[7] Put in Gramscian terms, the cinematic image culled from this distorted memory (nostalgia) creates a kind of misguided "good sense," one that leads us to understand Italian Americans only in stereotypes—stereotypes, I should add, that tend to reinforce racial and sexual hierarchies, supporting a status-quo hegemony. When, instead, we look in an engaged and informed way for images of common sense, as we might call them, in films depicting Italian American experiences, we are more likely to distinguish between those and other more limiting images.

In her survey of the cinematic treatment of Italian American women, Francesca Canadé Sautman finds characters that are what Jacqueline Reich has described as "the sensuous bombshell à la Sophia Loren or the overbearing Italian mamma" (11).[8] As Sautman explains: "Most [Italian American] women in films have thus been presented as mammas tottering out of the kitchen or housewives who are also, in mob films, consumerist parasites, accessories to murder which fills their bank accounts" ([sic], Sautman 229). In addition to the abundance of these stock female Italian American characters, the labor of Italian American women is rarely shown. Even labor that would most likely be connected to the two generic categories of "madonnas and whores" rarely gets visualized on screen, particularly in big-budget Hollywood films.

In investigating this absence of women at work, Sautman correctly moves to a consideration of working-class culture and what she argues is a contradictory relationship between films and real life. She maintains that Italian Americans on screen are most often connected to working-class culture regardless of the time period of the film's narrative. Furthermore, when they are not associated with the working class, they are gangsters: "Indeed, most Italian Americans in film are assumed to be lower class/working class, wealth and comfort stem solely from a life of crime" (229). Moving away from the Italian-as-gangster image, other films emphasize working-class culture as a defining factor of Italian American identity. Thus we have films such as John

Turturro's *Mac*, Robert Mulligan's *Blood Brothers*, and Robert De Niro's *A Bronx Tale*, to name a few.

The problem with many such "working-class" films is that when Italian Americans are associated with working-class culture, a kind of narrative and visual nostalgic imagery exists that neglects female labor (inside or outside of the home) and ignores Italian American assimilation. That is, while a pro-labor message is ever present (even in many gangster films), the labor of women (waged or unwaged) is abundantly absent in films that depict Italian American experiences. This absence, especially when seen in films set in pre-1970s United States, oddly enough suggests a certain socioeconomic status whereby women did not need to work:

> The view still prevails that Italian women from South[ern Italy] were always chained to the stove and bedroom and hardly put their nose outside. This inaccurate picture, which Di Leonardo calls "the rhetoric of nostalgia," has been so pervasive among Italians because it idealizes the memories of a painful experience and implies a higher social status of informants who claim that the women in their families never had to work. . . . Popular film . . . has hastily endorsed the stereotypical images of ethnic nostalgia and practically shut women out of the work space, while at the same time, showing them, by definition, as vulgar and "lower class." (Sautman 228)

Such films paradoxically suggest that Italian American families are middle class, and yet mark them as nondominant or nonmainstream (hardworking laborers or criminals). Although "working-class" films go far in deconstructing the gangster myth and other powerful images also connected to the U.S. hegemonic culture, they also rearticulate the image of the macho, hardworking Italian laborer, a stereotype that while based in truth evades or ignores Italian Americans' assimilation and rise to the middle class (which did or did not carry with it a continuation of the macho, hard-working—albeit economically stable—Italian American *male*).

It is perhaps predictable that a discussion of cinematic images of Italian Americans and dominant U.S. culture would lead to some consideration of ethnic assimilation. It is not easy to summarize assimilation and socioeconomic mobility of Italian Americans—in part because of the different waves of immigration. Nonetheless, most historians recognize both the continued prevalence of an Italian American working class (mostly in northeastern cities), while exploring the many economic gains Italian Americans have made. The reasons for assimilation are equally difficult to pin down: Mangione and Morreale suggest rather simply that assimilation was caused by the "changing character and image of [Italian] immigrants—as perceived by themselves and by the world around them . . . the changing roles of women in and out of the family, as well as . . . the effects of two world wars" (325).[9] For my purposes, exploring the reasons for assimilation are less significant than examining assimilation itself alongside its on-screen version. While second-, third-, and fourth-generation Italians in North America have become more and more part of upper- and middle-class America, we see little parallel sign of this affluence in cinema. In fact, it is relatively safe to say that most white-collar Italian Americans in films are in some way connected to organized crime.

This cinematic rhetoric of nostalgia (cinematic images of the Italian American as either gangster or working stiff, both outside of mainstream, middle-class America) evades an acknowledgment of Italian American assimilation into the white social landscape of the United States. That is, it overlooks the development of how "Italians became white." The phrase "Italians became white" suggests a historical critique in line with one that references how Irish Americans became part of mainstream middle and upper classes and in so doing distanced themselves from other minority and immigrant groups.[10] The idea of Italian Americans in North America similarly "becoming white" is a multifaceted subject that deserves a much broader and more historically based intervention than my current project. One can look to, for example, the ground-breaking collection, *Are Italians White? How Race Is Made in America*, edited by Jennifer Guglielmo and Salvatore Salerno, for sustained, historically relevant work on the subject. There are many ways of thinking about the process of Italian Americans becoming white. In fact, claiming it as a process, rather than an always-already accepted fact or fiction, is merely one position on the topic.[11] The theme, though, of forgetting runs as a connective thread through many discussions of Italian Americans and whiteness, as Guglielmo suggests in the introductory essay to *Are Italians White?* "Italians were not always white, and the loss of this memory is one of the tragedies of racism in America" (1). It is exactly this loss, associated with the rhetoric of nostalgia discussed above, that we can trace cinematically. The repeated visual/cinematic elision of the process of Italian American assimilation paradoxically asserts Italian Americans as "ethnic" by linking them to the working or criminal class and erasing the work of women.

Therefore, many films about Italian American gangster and working-class culture reinforce the assimilation of Italian Americans not through the conventional representation of social homogenization (where markers of difference are gradually erased) but rather through the hypervisibility of Italian American uniqueness (their exaggerated ethnicity). This uniqueness, it seems necessary to repeat, tends to overlook the ways in which Italian Americans have become white and middle class. Put differently, such films exaggerate Italian American identity to the point of caricature and thereby whitewash the complexities of assimilation. Instead, certain cinematic perspectives, "mediated versions" of reality (to evoke Stam again), highlight the working lives of Italian American women. In so doing, they strategically rely on experiences of common sense, folklore, and the basic daily routines of life in order to depict a sense of Italian American identity that moves beyond rigid stereotypes and thus moves toward a more nuanced national popular culture. Even though the lives of these characters are themselves sometimes rendered in broad strokes, they nevertheless remain recognizably "human."

Women in Italian American Hollywood Films

Since the 1970s, Francis Ford Coppola and Martin Scorsese have been lauded by sometimes divergent groups as being the cinematic spokesmen for Italians in the United States (see Casillo 374–375, in Tamburri et al.). Countless Italian American social organizations and academics have both recognized them as exemplary of all Italian Americans and condemned their stereotypical depictions of Italian Americans as criminals and gangsters. Although the association of Italians in the United States with mobster life had already been well demarcated by Hollywood films before Coppola and Scorsese, they are often credited with being the first and most talented Italian American directors to make films explicitly about Italians' experiences (mob-related or otherwise) in the United States. They are commended for working within the parameters of Hollywood conventions, but altering, adjusting, and perhaps even deconstructing previous stereotypes; simultaneously they are criticized for rearticulating and reinforcing those same stereotypes.

While there were plenty of Italian gangster films before *The Godfather*, Coppola's film based on Mario Puzo's best-selling novel, paved the way, for even more mafia-focused films by directors such as Scorsese, Brian DePalma, John Huston, and Jonathan Demme as well as the more recent television phenomenon of David Chase's *The Sopranos*. Written in part in a beatnik coffee shop in San Francisco's North Beach, Caffé Trieste (a picture of Puzo and Coppola writing is proudly displayed next to such cultural icons as Claudio Villa and Don Novello, a.k.a. Father Guido Sarducci, on the café's walls), *The Godfather* examines the alternative structure of an Old World way of living that found the resources and systems of the White-Anglo-Saxon-Protestant New World uninviting, if not downright threatening. The line between public official laws and underworld mafia laws are blurred, and the formal structure, images, and narrative encourage the audience to sympathize with the Italians—who are, after all, immigrants merely trying to cut out their piece of the American dream under sometimes challenging circumstances.

This praise aside, *The Godfather* passes over many significant details in the lives and power struggles of the mafiosi and their families.[12] In the first place, the film ignores an important historical lesson about some of the reasons that led to the formation of such an underground world in the United States, an absence that was later explained (nonetheless problematically) by *The Godfather: Part II*, which chronicles Vito Corleone's life in Sicily and New York City before he became Don.[13] The other significant gap is a strange absence of women and children in a film whose main (male) characters repeatedly state the importance of *la famiglia*. Some of the absences of women and children seem connected to the use of specific camera movements and editing choices that heighten narrative parallels and produce drama. One such sequence, which relies on parallel close-ups and match cuts for dramatic effect, is the suggestive closing baptism scene, where the soon-to-be-crowned Don, Michael Corleone, stands as his nephew's godfather. Medium and close-up shots of Michael's renouncement of Satan (a necessary part of the sacrament of baptism) are cross-cut with similar shots of his men killing the leaders of the five rival families in a visual montage that at once affirms Michael's commitment to his church and family and hypocritically comments on the violence on which that commitment must be based. In the moment that he becomes godfather to his nephew, he is also taking his father's place as the godfather to his extended family's business. Nonetheless, the attention to detail (albeit often stylized) manifest throughout the film, but in particular during the baptismal ceremony, is completely undermined by the lack of a godmother for the baby. If the scene's authenticity is secured by, for instance, a Latin mass, why not a godmother? While Michael's wife, Kay, holds the baby, we do not watch or hear her renounce Satan. (Not to mention the fact that we never learn anything about Kay's own conversion to Catholicism from Protestantism, something Puzo's novel narrates.) Women are not, in the Coppola version of Italian American life, participants in either the commitment to the church or the family.

Stylistic and visual parallels aside, the Don's daughter, Connie, who marries Carlo as the film opens, is also absent throughout much of the film. While her brother Sonny shows genuine alarm over the abuse she receives from her husband, once Sonny is killed we do not see Connie again until the end of the film. By then, we have learned that Carlo's wife-beating was only a ploy to rile up Sonny. Connie, nonetheless, was an abused pregnant woman, whose situation is skipped over for more tragic, though not more dramatic, moments. After we see the pregnant and bruised Connie, the scene cuts quickly to Sonny's murder, and then back to Sicily for the murder of Michael's first wife, Appollonia. Connie, in fact, only appears again near the end of the film as the hysterical "Bertha," presumably drugged to calm down what the family sees as a psychotic belief that Michael had her husband killed (something he did indeed do). Connie is comforted by the naïve Kay, who, throughout the film (and on into *The Godfather: Part II*), acts as an outsider looking in, a narrative device that helps the rest of us understand the details of organized crime.

Interestingly, Kay is the only woman shown working (outside of domestic duties)—we see her briefly working as an elementary school teacher before she marries Michael. This absence is not surprising since the women in the narrative are all married to the mob, and their husbands' positions in the family business mean the women do not have to work for a wage, allowing more time, one might think, for creating a domestic haven for their families. This being said, the Italian mamma in the kitchen—an otherwise central and widespread image—is practically nonexistent in *The Godfather*. The film denies women even this form of labor. This erasure, along with the family's continued criminal lifestyle, creates a cinematic rhetoric of nostalgia, an intentional deviation from accuracy, to heighten the popular appeal of the narrative.[14]

The absence of a recognition of women's labor is particularly startling when we look at images of food and its preparation. Numerous gangster films have scenes in which men are cooking or talking about cooking. As mentioned above, midway through Scorsese's *Goodfellas*, Henry Hill goes into great detail describing meals he and his fellow gangsters prepared while incarcerated, recalling, in particular, the meticulous method Paulie had for slicing garlic. Toward the end of the film, we again hear Henry describe a multicourse meal, this time the one we watch him prepare for his family as he frantically tries to take care of a drug deal. Further, on different occasions throughout the film the camera lingers on Paulie in front of a grill or frying pan cooking Italian sausages.

The relationship between Italian American gangsters and food is so strong in a film such as *Goodfellas*, one wonders how these hardened and ironically named racketeers learned to cook. My immediate (somewhat anecdotally based) answer is, well, they must have learned to cook from their mothers and grandmothers. Yet in Scorsese's adaptation of the real Pileggi's *Wiseguy*, women are rarely, if ever, visually connected to food. In fact, Henry comments once or twice that he does not let his wife Karen cook since she is not any good at it—after all, like Kay Adams, she is not Italian American. As it is, the goodfellas did not learn to cook in their mothers' kitchens, but rather, in prison.[15]

Gangster films, especially from *The Godfather* on, again and again feature scenes in which men in prison and men hiding out after a hit cook for themselves.[16] Indeed, one is led to reason that it was in these spaces—barred cells and smoky poolrooms—that such wiseguys learned how to sauté onions and garlic properly for a sauce or test to see if their pasta is *al dente*. Sautman also details some of the instances in Italian American cinema in which we find imprisoned or on-the-lam mobsters behind the stove. She has observed, further, that food is, again and again, connected to a masculine, mobster environment: Food is an "unmistakable signature of things Italian apposed to mob life" (235). Pasta and spaghetti, in particular, are connected to gangsters. Sautman shows this connection by describing the common imagery: "gangsters amorously stirring deep red meat sauces between hits, and as blood is splattered everywhere, red pasta sauce explodes on the screen too" (235).

Not only do we see men cooking multicourse meals for themselves, but sometimes they give cooking lessons to other, younger mobsters, creating a kind of male domestic genealogy—godfathers teaching goodfellas how to cook. Returning to *The Godfather*, we can find such a lineage, for instance, in the kitchen of the Corleone family, where Clemenza gives the Don-apparent, Michael Corleone, a quick lesson in making ragù while the men discuss plans to avenge the hit on their father.[17]

The only scene where women are cooking in *The Godfather* clearly displays how women's labor and contributions to the home are ignored, a distortion that at once acts to strengthen the relationship between men and cooking and to sustain an image of upper-middle-class women who do not cook. When we see women cooking (when the Don comes home from the hospital) the camera is placed at such an oblique angle in the kitchen, that we barely get a glimpse of Mamma Corleone's chicken cacciatore before a cut to the Don's sick bed. The soundtrack barely registers the mostly inaudible kitchen banter between the four women and their children, who are crowded in the screen, up against two walls of the kitchen, their backs to the camera. The shot is in fact from the perspective of the kitchen door, from the perspective, one could assume, of a (perhaps male) outsider who cannot quite decipher the kitchen space. A few minutes later around the dinner table, even the fruits of their labor are not given any screen time, because of the setup of the shot. The family sits around the dining room table with Sonny and Mamma Corleone at the two heads, but Mamma's back faces the camera again (like in the kitchen), and her body blocks the view of the food on the table. The camera angle, though, allows a generally unobstructed view of

Sonny at the center of the discussion. When we look back at the earlier cooking lesson in the same kitchen with Clemenza and Michael, the obstruction of women and women's work becomes even more obvious. In that earlier scene where Clemenza teaches Michael how to cook ragù, the kitchen is in full view and the camera moves freely around the room directed at the other men. It is as though the scopophilic "man behind the camera" more comfortably moves around the room when there are only men in the kitchen—whereas when women are in the kitchen, it becomes a foreign space.

Extending this interpretation a bit leads us to see the Corleone kitchen as a flexible space, what Edward Soja might call a thirdspace. Soja introduces thirdspace by giving it an "evolving definition," one which involves "the creation of another mode of thinking about space . . . [that] is simultaneously real and imagined and more . . . the exploration of Thirdspace can be described and inscribed in journeys to 'real-and-imagined' . . . places" (11).[18] For men in the mob, the kitchen becomes an acceptable space for their labors when incarcerated or in some kind of self-isolating circumstance. The kitchen becomes a thirdspace, because contradictory actions and labors can function simultaneously within it. The gangsters' exaggerated machismo and tendency to violence intertwines with their domesticated, sensitive, homosocial actions whereby they act out traditionally female tasks. The Italian American gangster film genre, as illustrated by my brief readings of *The Godfather* and *Goodfellas*, and Italian American films generally, reinforce the rhetoric of nostalgia by simultaneously obfuscating women's labors, underscoring male domesticity, and highlighting an Italian American culture that remains outside of white, mainstream U.S. culture.

Stepping away from cinema for a moment, we can look to at least one of Puzo's other novels in order to get a different perspective on gender, labor, immigration, and the world of organized crime. His 1964 *The Fortunate Pilgrim* "received critical acclaim without financial success," as Gardaphè puts it in his *Leaving Little Italy* (34). Puzo's focus on the entire family, but in particular on the mother, Lucia Santa (not to mention Octavia, her daughter), is noteworthy. He constructs complex female characters and thus presents us with a depiction of an Italian immigrant woman that was not terribly common in the early 1960s, especially in writings by male authors. But it is not so much that Puzo offers us, in Lucia Santa, a feminist Italian American literary character (we should look elsewhere for such female characterizations); rather, it is that Puzo gives us a figure who stands out quite dramatically when compared to similar, albeit less central, figures who appear in the author's more widely read novel, *The Godfather*.[19] While Puzo's *The Godfather* offers a more balanced view of women than the film version, its success is in great part due to those aspects of the narrative (organized crime and the folk culture that exists around it) that are most connected to a false "good sense," or rhetoric of nostalgia.

Tarantella: Dancing about History

Perhaps no other film does more to connect food and its preparation to Italian American women than independent filmmaker Helen de Michiels's 1995 *Tarantella*.[20] In *Tarantella* we have a vision of women and labor powerfully connected to the home and its environment in such a way as to make that relationship—home-food-woman—a positive, alternative space for the recognition of women's history and immigrant identity. Going beyond a simple visual or narrative celebration of women working in the home, de Michiel, in what we could call a Gramscian approach, uses experimental narrative forms and historical specificity to create a meaningful way of understanding Italian American women. De Michiel's exploration of Italian American women's labor within the home critiques the rhetoric of nostalgia by producing a narrative that recognizes Italian American assimilation into middle-class, white culture, thereby recuperating as historically significant the unwaged domestic labor of Italian American women. In addition to intervening on the paradigm that ignores female labor, the film's emphasis on the kitchen and the work related to it acts to critique stereotypes about Italian American women as kerchiefed mammas, wooden spoon in hand. By taking back the kitchen, de Michiel recuperates it as a liberating space. Paradoxically, however, by focusing on the private, domestic space of the kitchen and the unwaged "homemaker" labor connected to this space, de Michiel also reaffirms the position of her protagonist, Diana di Sorella, as part of the dominant, white middle class. On the other hand, it is because of the liberating potential of the kitchen (and Diana's recognition that private and public spaces are interrelated) that alliances are formed (albeit provisional in some cases) with other women.

Diana represents an Italian American woman at the end of the twentieth century. Systematically dispelling stereotypes, Diana claims for herself a kind of identity that is instilled with her mother's past but looks forward.[21] Through Diana's memory and recollection, the film recognizes the hardships of her family's immigrant past but does not claim victimization or oppression. Most importantly, it subtly recognizes Diana's privilege as an assimilated white woman of Italian descent—a privilege that gives her the freedom to explore her family's past and to find purpose and meaning in the household labor of her mother and grandmother.

The simple plot of *Tarantella* does little to explain the film's alternative narrative potential, but upon closer inspection we find that the film establishes a national popular culture, developed with the help of an organic intellectual and through attention to the everyday experiences and folk culture of female immigrant domestic life. Diana, a professional photographer, works as an artist and lives with her non-Italian, white boyfriend, Matt. She returns to her old Italian American urban neighborhood when her mother, Silvia, dies. In addition to the practical business of taking care of her mother's things and selling her family's home, Diana must also come to terms with her family's immigrant background and her Italian American ethnicity, a subjectivity, we learn quickly, Diana has almost purposefully tried to forget.

Over an all-too-brief period, Diana develops a friendship with her mother's friend, Pina, who, acting as a kind of surrogate mother/organic intellectual to Diana, helps her recognize her place in a female genealogy and to appreciate her immigrant past. More than a general history, Pina teaches Diana a female history based on food, domestic work, and storytelling. By pointing out how the women in Diana's family created a specific Sicilian-American environment, Pina helps Diana see where she stands with respect to the women in her family and, in so doing, underscores the significance of a common sense notion of the world. Pina's series of stories emphasize folk culture and peasant, subaltern practices, even when these come at the expense of women's independence and livelihood. Although the story she retells includes vicious patriarchy and maltreatment of women, Pina also teaches Diana to see creativity within unwaged domestic labor and to recognize the freedom that can be experienced and obtained within the home. Thus, Pina acts as a guide for Diana, organically illustrating the importance of folk culture and domesticity in the formation of identity.

Each aspect of Pina's history lesson comes together in the form of a "dream book" or *libro della casa*, a scrap book/diary/cookbook that Diana's mother (and before her, her grandmother) lovingly created. Images of cooking and descriptions of recipes repeatedly give meaning to the storyline and help Diana recall and reconsider aspects of the ethnic childhood she has forgotten or ignored. While much of Pina's history lessons to Diana is shown to us through standard cinematic techniques, a large part of the narrative unfolds in a storytelling technique dramatized by traditional Italian marionettes. (That Italy has a long tradition of marionettes suggests ways de Michiel is evoking a kind of artisan folk culture as well.) The puppet aspect of the film, intercut with Diana's conversations with Pina, tells a straight narrative—a story of Diana's grandmother's life in Italy and why she came to America. Within the narrative is a description of how the *libro della casa* (*libro*) came into existence. The entire *libro* is written in Italian, a language with which Diana is only barely familiar. Pina makes the language accessible to Diana, bridging the gap between the subaltern and dominant cultures, as would an organic intellectual. The marionettes, then, form the visual interpretation of Pina's translation and further add to the way in which this film adopts folk ways to create a sustainable and flexible national popular culture.

The film relies on two nontraditional cinematic narrative techniques that together construct a narrative opposed to more conventional films featuring Italian American families and thus offer an alternative perception of Italian American women to those of contemporary popular culture stereotypes. One nontraditional cinematic technique employed is the use of the Italian marionettes to tell Diana's grandmother's story; the other is the use of flashbacks and daydream sequences in which Diana appears, sometimes as an adult, sometimes as a child, contemplating her past or the past of her mother and grandmother.

The daydream/flashback moments act both as a visual image of Diana's memories and as a means for deconstructing stereotypes about Italian and Italian American women. For instance, she recalls moments of her childhood, such as reading children's books in Italian or making cookies with her mother and grandmother. Such realistic sequences are juxtaposed with sequences that take on a more fantastical effect. Through visual creations of Diana's thoughts, de Michiel intervenes (often ironically) on stereotypes and traditional roles associated with Italian women. For example, in two related daydream sequences, Diana renegotiates her position as an Italian American woman by challenging archetypal images of Italian women. In both sequences the adult Diana and the child Diana, respectively, stand as actresses in what seems to be a photo shoot for an advertisement for De Cecco-brand pasta. They are the "De Cecco girls"—the female embodiment of perfect pasta—dressed in *contadina*-style clothes, with scarves in their hair and holding grain. They both fidget and refuse to stand for the photographer, and when the young Diana is on the set, she mockingly bites into a *cannolo*, playing up her ethnic roots to the point of an exaggerated parody.[22] The majority of these flashback and daydream sequences contain references to photography and other creative depictions of reality (not surprising considering Diana's profession). The use of photography within the visual interpretations of Diana's thoughts emphasizes her struggle to understand a past that only seems accessible to her through mediated realities.

At its most basic, the film tells a female history. It emphasizes ways women create and carry on culture, through cooking, story telling, and artistry, and reinforces these actions through the visual impact of the *libro*, an artistic and historical record of the history of the women in Diana's family. The *libro* acts as a historical record, outside of dominant forms of documentation. Oddly enough, at first, Diana, an artist by profession, does not even understand its importance—she does not recognize it as either art or history. Yet, as she learns (and recalls what she already knew) about Italian American female domesticity, she recognizes the *libro* as a necessary part of her own formation. The *libro* becomes a site, a visual interpretation of common sense we might say, for recuperating a past obscured by Diana's assimilation and stereotypes of Italian Americans. By extension, this site intervenes on the cinematic rhetoric of nostalgia, because it underscores the importance of Italian American women's labor and implicitly documents Italian Americans' movement into the middle class.

Nevertheless, we should be quick to recognize that it is in part because of Diana's position as a white, middle-class woman that she has the privilege to explore her immigrant roots, parody the stereotypes related to them, and most importantly, recognize the kitchen (and its unwaged labor) as a liberating space. While Pina comes to Diana's aid and acts as a kind of organic intellectual, interpreting folk culture and language for her, it would be especially misguided to call Diana a subaltern. In spite of Diana's advantages, she implicitly looks beyond this privileged perspective by the alliances (however temporary) suggested with other women. Through such gendered alliances she recognizes the kitchen as part of the public, economic system, and thus inadvertently or not makes a Gramscian theoretical move.

Her exploration of her immigrant past through the *libro* culminates in her gendered alliances with Pina. What's more, Diana also forms a relationship with the young South Asian girl in the airport sitting with her parents. Through a close-up shot-reaction-shot Diana and the unnamed girl make eye contact. Diana, we might hope, recognizes that her situation is different than that of this immigrant family; yet the formal elements of the sequence (the recognition and acknowledgment seen in the close-up shot-reaction-shot) suggests a provisional alliance. This provisional alliance calls to mind an acknowledgment of the contradictory relations with their cultures of origin and with globalization more generally. De Michiel does not, however, embrace a universalist model of multiculturalism. In fact, no stylistic or narrative similarities are created between, for instance, Diana and the young Latino gay couple who are looking to buy her mother's house, the young Italian American male bartender, or the middle-aged Italian American man in the neighborhood—de Michiel, it seems, is most concerned with the potential for alliances with other women. De Michiel's subtle parallels between Diana and other women in the narrative suggest a potential for future alliances that could uncover and interpret other forms of erasures or marginalizations. Though remaining only on the level of potentiality, such a film then, establishes a flexible kind of national popular culture (similar to the idea of an international popular culture I discuss elsewhere), one that recognizes the role of immigrant women in the formation of culture generally.

Buying into *Household Saints*

Like *Tarantella*, Nancy Savoca's 1993 *Household Saints* explores the effect of assimilation on the culture of Italian American families. While *Tarantella* seems to recuperate the kitchen as a liberating space and to suggest, however vaguely, possible gendered alliances, *Household Saints* offers an ambiguous commentary on the idea of the kitchen as a liberating space. Savoca's not-quite independent film questions if the movement of Italian Americans into a consumerist, middle-class life in the 1950s and 1960s helped liberate Italian American women from Old World-patriarchal constraints or merely reinstituted those constraints within a dominant, nonethnic environment.[23] Aaron Baker and Julian Vitullo reach a similar conclusion: "*Household Saints* questions whether the Americanization and consumerism that had infiltrated Italian/American life helped liberate women from the 'superstitions' of traditional culture or rather reproduced the same contradictions" (56). The film takes a Gramscian-style approach to critiquing the private space of family and domesticity versus the seemingly public space of waged labor and consumerism. It emphasizes folk culture and common sense, in much the same way as *Tarantella*, but it makes a particularly strong visual comparison between the dominant culture and that of the immigrant family. It recognizes the interdependence of public (read: dominant) and private (read: subaltern) spaces by following the assimilation of one family who keeps hold of certain markers of their immigrant past. The choice about what aspects of immigrant culture to keep or discard is determined by the women in the family. More specifically still, each woman's relationship to domestic labor helps shape the family's overall relationship to a dominant, middle-class white American identity.

The narrative follows three generations of Italian American women living in New York (first-generation Carmela Santangelo; her daughter-in-law, Catherine; and Catherine's daughter, Teresa), focusing mainly on the second and third generation (Catherine and Teresa). When each woman's history is unraveled in relation to the other, the greater story recounted is one of a constant battle between specifically Italian folk attitudes and values and mainstream American ones, thus walking a fine line between common sense and good sense. The different ways in which each woman chooses to continue or stop certain immigrant traditions and activities marks her family members' sometimes contradictory assimilation patterns as ethnic whites into a dominant middle-class American culture.

The three women have very different responses to the dominant culture. For Carmela, all things not Italian are to be shunned and kept at a distance. Even in her old age, Carmela continues to make sausages for the family butcher shop and to act as a spiritual leader and mystic for her family. She resists assimilation by enforcing Italian folk traditions, or common sense, within and outside her immediate household.[24] Yet she makes certain concessions for the sake of getting by and making a living. For instance, the family butcher shop sells turkeys for Thanksgiving to nonethnic white housewives (who make special shopping trips to the exotic Italian neighborhood to get the freshly killed birds), but Carmela does not actually celebrate the holiday. Carmela, however, unconsciously deploys common sense when it profits her and her family but is unable to recognize when her folk values may be keeping her family from cultural stability (let alone upper mobility).

The character of Catherine is juxtaposed with that of her mother-in-law, Carmela, in such a way that we see Gramsci's ideas of common sense and good sense working with and against each other. Throughout her life, Catherine attempts (only sometimes successfully) to marry her traditional duties as an Italian American woman with the mores of the greater American culture outside of her neighborhood—mores that slowly seep into her community. She is, in fact, introduced to us as a typical star-struck teenager of post–World War II America, one who is more concerned with reading movie magazines than learning how to prepare antipasto, lasagna, and veal for the man her father has arranged for her to marry.[25]

It does not take Catherine long to recognize, however, that she can choose which traditions to carry on and which traditions will not function well within a community that is constantly moving toward a more consumerist middle-class culture. In short, Catherine illustrates a successful and self-conscious use of common sense in the face of dominant culture. Baker and Vitullo note that "the conflict between an urban Italian/American neighborhood in decline and the developing suburbs of the post-war period looms in the background of the entire film," and yet it is Catherine who seems best equipped to negotiate these conflicting pressures (63). At times confused, Catherine ultimately becomes the most sensible woman on screen—recognizing the importance of keeping certain traditions while discarding those that only keep her and her family ignorant or mark them as outsiders or immigrants. For instance, when she takes over making the sausages after Carmela dies, she continues reciting the innocuous recipe/incantation that her mother-in-law always repeated. Yet after her miscarriage (which Carmela had blamed on a curse) she reads up on pregnancy and human anatomy in order to prove that certain Old World ideas are outdated, misinformed folklore, which only act to keep her and her family from fully participating in an economically mobile culture. In fact, in this way Catherine has been quite capable at bridging the cultural gap between her immigrant (read: subaltern) positionality and her assimilated one.

Baker and Vitullo argue that Catherine discards those aspects of Italian culture sustained by women: "Rather than depending on Italian traditions created and maintained by women, Catherine relies on the advice of books that preach self-determination through medical knowledge, and gives birth in a hospital rather than with a midwife [as she did with her first child]" (58). Yet Catherine's relationship to assimilation is slightly more complex—after Carmela dies she puts away her mother-in-law's cross, votives, and Madonna statues but sends her daughter, Teresa, to Catholic school; she mocks Carmela's ideas about curses and the power of the evil eye but continues to use her recipe/incantation in order to make perfect sausages. In these examples, it would seem that she discards Old World traditions with respect to her private, domestic space (pregnancy and redecorating the house) but holds on to them in relation to what are seemingly public spaces (the sausages she makes to be sold and sending Teresa to Catholic school). In another sense, her decisions about what traditions to continue demonstrate the flexibility of private and public space, and illustrate how the two spaces are in fact arbitrarily demarcated and falsely separated. It is not so much that she rejects "her family's feminized Old World legacy" in light of a "new American identity," as Baker and Vitullo argue, but that her conscious acceptance of a consumer culture both within and beyond a strict domestic sphere illustrates her and her family's movement to a position of mainstream middle-class America. Baker and Vitullo describe the visuals that link these ideas; we hear

> Catherine's voice reading a list of "Old World Wives' Tales" from a modern medical text, [and] we see her redecorating Carmela's room and returning from a shopping spree, heavy with child and packages, to a kitchen full of new appliances. (58)

Savoca chronicles assimilation in full bloom and explicitly connects it to a capitalist and consumerist culture.

Unlike Catherine, who is still linked to immigrant culture even though she moves toward assimilation, Teresa, her daughter, seems unable to function within a family that has combined an approach to assimilation with a continued reverence for specific aspects of Italian immigrant culture. The story of Catherine and her daughter, Teresa, almost overwhelms that of Carmela, and thus the film can almost be understood as two separate narratives (Catherine's story ends soon after Teresa is born). The break in the film, cinematically constructed with an abrupt flash forward to Teresa at eight years old, reinforces the generational change. Until this point, the narrative slowly jumped by months and years; the second half of the film jumps first to Teresa at eight, then as a young teen, and finally at about nineteen or twenty (set in 1970). These somewhat jarring temporal movements parallel the family's fast-paced movement into the middle class. Catherine's actions continue to be the best markers of the family's change. By the time Teresa is in high school, her mother seems to cook meat and potatoes exclusively and is convincing Joseph that they should send Teresa to college—she can become a teacher, Catherine suggests, "It'll give her something to do until she gets married." While Joseph is not easily convinced—in fact, we never know for sure that he would have agreed to send Teresa to college)—it is clear that Catherine is by now more comfortable negotiating their multicultural world. Furthermore, Catherine stands in contradistinction to Teresa, who seems unable to function within a household where American middle-class attitudes and Italian immigrant folk traditions cohabitate.

Indeed, Teresa clearly embodies the fanatical piety of the immigrant grandmother she never knew. Like Carmela, Teresa becomes a devout Catholic; yet, unlike Carmela, who saw domestic labor as a duty and sausage-making as a way to make a living (which needed spiritual help to be successful), Teresa explicitly links her spirituality only to unwaged domestic labor. As a child, she unconsciously links household chores with her devout practice of religion; as a teenager, she learns about the life of her namesake, St. Therese, "the little flower," and decides to live her life as the saint lived hers, dedicating herself, as her voiceover narration tells us, "to all the little things that go unnoticed, unacknowledged and unappreciated"; thus she obsessively relines the family's kitchen drawers with butcher paper and scrubs her boyfriend's toaster with a toothbrush. Teresa, similar to her grandmother, embodies an unconscious use of common sense. She links her Old World spiritual values to unwaged labor but lives in a world that doesn't value such labor; thus she suffers from a kind of cognitive dissonance.

When Teresa desires to become a Carmelite nun are thwarted by her father, she becomes more devoted to living her life like St. Therese. Her religious fervor to perform domestic labor reaches a climax when she has a vision of Jesus as she irons her boyfriend's shirt. This cinematic magical realism moment creates a visual parallel with Carmela's earlier visions of her dead husband and further strengthens the two women's similarities. Interestingly, in this moment—when Teresa's work is most powerfully linked to both her spirituality and her resistance to her father's commands—Savoca sends a rather ambiguous message, one Baker and Vitullo describe (perhaps with an intentional pun) as irony: "The everyday task of ironing is therefore elevated into a divine act of service to others, yet not without irony. Christ expresses his appreciation for Teresa's work by providing her with hundreds of similar red-checkered shirts to keep her busy the entire day" (59). Her visions and obsessive cleaning, interpreted as a delusional psychosis by everyone, continue when her parents place her in a rest home, where she scrubs the floors and talks about playing pinochle with God.

When Teresa unexpectedly dies, her father is the first one to name her a saint, immediately noticing that she smells like roses and that the hospital's garden, dead the day before, was now in full bloom. Catherine tries to convince him otherwise, suggesting once again her more deep-rooted assimilation: She argues simply that Teresa "went crazy ironing her boyfriend's shirts." Back in their neighborhood mysticism still reigns, and Teresa ascends to a level of sainthood in her community. A myth around her and her family begins, and from then on Joseph Santangelo's sausages are thought to cure the sick and aid the needy. The reverence Teresa receives in death by others reinforces the values she lived by and raises the significance of "all the little things" she did in life. Indeed death has transformed her (through her connection to the sausages) into an easily-exchangeable commodity.

The film does not end on this high note, however, but instead offers a more even-handed—although ambiguous—closing scene. This sequence at once encapsulates the histories of all three women and reaffirms the generational changes effected by migration. In fact, the film's ambiguous overall message—did the movement of Italian American families into a consumerist middle class help women or merely reinstitute patriarchal customs?—is strengthened by a framing device that loosely holds the narrative together. The closing sequence refers to the beginning of the film and creates a frame through which to view the women's stories. The framing story places the narrative in the early 1990s, in the backyard of an unnamed family eating sausages. The sausage functions as a memento, jarring the old man and woman to tell the younger generations at the table about the delicious, healing Santangelo sausages, which some say had been blessed by the dead Teresa. The old man then begins to recount how Joseph Santangelo, some forty years earlier, had won his wife, Catherine, in a pinochle game, and thus the story of Carmela, Catherine, and Teresa begins. At the end of the film we are brought back to the family, now finishing its lunch. The old woman finishes the story her husband had started earlier and comments on the relationship between domesticity and spirituality: "The grandmother . . . ends the story by stressing the divinity of the domestic through her assertion that Teresa 'saw God in her work'" (Baker and Vitullo 66). Such an affirmation suggests that the film defines labor connected to the domestic space of the kitchen as liberating and sees a balance existing between Italian American and dominant cultures. Yet their daughter, a baby in her arms, offers another perspective, a view that emphasizes the effect of domestic work on Italian American families and assimilation. The perspective of the woman with child critiques domesticity and unwaged household labor as a defining factor for women: "I could name a list of women as long as my arm who went crazy cooking and cleaning and trying to please everybody." The film then ends with a tablecloth covering the screen as wine that was spilled on it is shaken off. In the closing shot of the film Savoca employs a totemic household item to suggest a stage's curtain, a striking image that lends a bold domestic theatricality to the entire narrative.

Savoca does not offer a single perspective on Italian American women's experiences; rather she complicates the history of Italian American women by recognizing the sometimes divergent effects of migration and assimilation on the everyday culture of Italian American families. Her search begins and ends in the present and recognizes that the past cannot be entirely recuperated or nostalgically relived—only remembered through mediated sources. Thus, like de Michiel's film, *Household Saints* dramatically represents the operations of national popular culture: Both films seek to express realities of the underrepresented and by extension foster a cultural representation and popular history based on those experiences.

Both Savoca and de Michiel offer an alternative vision of Italian American women's experiences. Reich's comments on Savoca's films apply neatly to de Michiel's work as well:

> with a subtle yet powerful touch, Savoca's films offer up portrayals of Italian American women who rise above . . . stereotypes, providing unique insights into issues of gender and ethnicity. The female characters who dominate her films give voice and vision to this less-heard and less-seen side of Italian American experience. (11)

Household Saints and *Tarantella* imagine, in very different ways, how Italian American women's experiences function in relation to the history of Italians in the United States and the often stereotype-laden discourse that depicts that history.

Their films raise new questions, not the least of which for our purposes is not where did the goodfellas learn to cook, but is the kitchen the only liberating space for Italian American women? Furthermore, these films, through their acknowledgment of Italian American assimilation, invite comparisons with narrative films on experiences of other immigrant women. Such comparisons may lead to the creation of a national popular culture that acknowledges the complexities of immigrant life as well as make way for the kind of alliances barely suggested in a film like *Tarantella*. Making visible the relationship between film and documented history illustrates how one influences the other. Examinations of ethnicity, gender, class, and the racialization of groups in the United States leads to a more nuanced understanding of both the role played by Italian Americans in the complex process of cultural homogenization and the stakes of wholesale assimilation.

Notes

1. The Henry Hill in Nicholas Pileggi's nonfiction narrative *Wiseguy*, as well as Scorsese's infamous one, is half Sicilian and half Irish.

2. The term "cryptoethnic" was coined by Linda Hutcheon in discussing a generation of women academics, herself included, who took their husbands' names when they married and consequently "hid" their ethnicity by using a non-Italian last name. See Hutcheon's article in Kenneth A. Ciongoli and Jay Parini's *Beyond the Godfather*.

3. As this book goes to press, Fred Gardaphè's *From Wiseguys to Wise Men: The Gangster and Italian American Masculinities* was released—it is a study that explores the image of the gangster in relation to masculinity.

4. For historical information on Italian immigration to North America see Absalom, Candelora, Clark, and Di Scala. Some general issues on migration are covered in the introduction to this book. Generally speaking, the largest group of Italian immigrants came between 1880 and 1930, and the second-largest group of people came in the post–World War II years. Women usually emigrated with or soon after husbands, brothers, or fathers.

5. For historical and ethnographic studies of Italian American women working in the United States see Donna R. Gabaccia, Nancy L. Green, Louise C. Odencrantz, Miriam Cohen, Micaela di Leonardo, and Paola A. Sensi-Isolani and Phylis C. Martinelli. See also an oral, transcribed, autobiography, *Rosa, the Life of an Italian Immigrant* (by Marie Hall Ets) about an Italian woman living and working in turn-of-the-century Chicago, and Idanna Pucci's *The Trials of Maria Barbella*, which recounts the story of an Italian immigrant who worked in New York City sweatshops in the 1890s and who became the first woman sentenced to the electric chair.

6. Gramsci's common sense (as opposed to good sense) has on the surface a regressive connotation in that it suggests the subalterns' ability to know and understand primarily only their own subaltern world. At the same time, Gramsci emphasizes each individual's potential to have an abstract and broad philosophical perspective, one that uses common sense informed by good sense; seen in this light, common sense becomes part of counter-hegemonic cultural practices. See the introduction for further discussion of Gramsci's common sense.

7. One should recall that Gramsci's ideas are somewhat limiting when it comes to film, for when he spoke of the development of national popular culture, he favored print culture over visual culture.

8. Jacqueline Reich in her "Nancy Savoca: An Appreciation" paraphrases Daniel Golden's comments on the "madonna/whore" dichotomy commonly associated with Italian American women (11).

9. They explain the changing roles of women mainly by noting that second- and third-generation Italian American women were given more educational opportunities and that more and more young men and women rejected their parents' attempts at "Old World" arranged marriages. They also point out (as do other historians, such as Cohen, Nelli, and di Leonardo) that between the 1950s and the 1970s, Italian American women moved from mainly working in factories to clerical jobs and "female-friendly" professions such as teaching and nursing. Italian American women's movement out of the factory parallels, of course, Italian Americans' movement, or rather, assimilation, into mainstream, dominant culture.

10. See, for instance, Noel Ignatiev's *How the Irish Became White*. See also numerous other studies on whiteness in relation to European immigration to the United States, including Matthew Frye Jacobson's *Whiteness of a Different Color*, Karen Brodkin's *How Jews Became White Folks and What That Says about Race in America*, or Grace Elizabeth Hale's *Making Whiteness*.

11. See Thomas A. Guglielmo's *White on Arrival* for a convincing argument that Italian immigrants, in many regards, became white the moment they set foot in the United States, although that white status did not always guarantee that they would not be discriminated against. While my discussion puts the whitening of Italians in a different context from that treated by Guglielmo, I view our work as complementary, even as we stress different aspects of Italian American history.

12. Nowhere in *The Godfather* is the word "mafia" used. In the 1977 television release of *The Godfather* and *The Godfather: Part II*, a prescreening disclaimer read: "*The Godfather* is a fictional account of the activities of a small group of ruthless criminals. It would be erroneous and unfair to suggest that they are representative of any ethnic group." For a discussion of this disclaimer see Carlos E. Cortés's "Italian-Americans in Film: From Immigrants to Icons."

13. My point here is not to read *The Godfather* trilogy in any great detail, but rather to use it as exemplary of a certain trend in U.S. cinema. I direct my readers to other considerations of Coppola's films that offer insightful readings of his work. See, for instance, Fred Gardaphè and Thomas J. Ferraro.

14. In *The Godfather*, Michael, a World War II veteran, initially resists becoming part of the family business but ultimately participates hoping to make the business "legitimate." Nonetheless, as much as the Corleones try (especially in *The Godfather: Part II* and *Part III*), they fail to assimilate completely to mainstream culture, and remain "criminals," who otherwise lead upper-middle-class lives.

15. Two noteworthy exceptions to this trend should be mentioned. First, in *Goodfellas*, Scorsese's mother, Catherine Scorsese, plays Joe Pesci's mother and serves the goodfellas a simple, late-night meal. Second, Scorsese's 1974 documentary, *Italianamerican*, is structured around his mother cooking spaghetti sauce and meatballs. The latter film, whose credits conclude with the recipe for the sauce, clearly demonstrates an acknowledgment of the importance of women's work in the home and also details a family's movement toward "bettering" itself, as Catherine Scorsese puts it.

16. Early gangster films, such as Mervyn LeRoy's 1930 *Little Casear*, link mobsters to an Italian American ethnicity through such details as eating (though not cooking) a plate of spaghetti.

17. Such a lineage also suggests Italian American cinema's organic connection with Italian neorealist cinema, in which father-son, male-male relationships typically enjoy narrative primacy. The male bonding so common within the gangster genre could easily be paralleled to the male bonding "buddy" relationships in Italian neorealist films. See my coedited *Italian Neorealism and Global Cinema* for expanded discussion of the male-male relationship in neorealism.

18. Elsewhere Soja comments on the transient nature of the term thirdspace, seeing it as "a purposefully tentative and flexible term that attempts to capture what is actually a constantly shifting and changing milieu of ideas, events, appearances, and meanings" (2).

19. Cataloguing strong female Italian American literary characters would be a hopelessly subjective, although highly diverting, project. One can start to get a sense of the scope of such an undertaking by first considering the creative and critical works of authors such as Helen Barolini, Mary Jo Bona, and Edvige Giunta.

20. I am grateful to Ben Lawton of Purdue University for his unpublished article on Helen de Michiel's *Tarantella* and to de Michiel for sending a copy of the film before it was available on tape.

21. See Lawton's article and Pasquale Verdicchio's Internet-published review of the film for other considerations of how it creates a story that counters Italian patriarchal traditions.

22. *Cannoli*, the ricotta-filled Sicilian sweets, are commonly used as emblematic of Italian (Sicilian) American culture (think of the famous "don't forget the *cannoli*" line in *The Godfather*). As Diana explores her family's past, Diana's boyfriend Matt explores all the clichéd traditions associated with Italian American city life. His time in Diana's family's house is spent listening to Frank Sinatra and Louis Prima records and going out to buy more and more *cannoli*. Yet even Matt manages to learn something about the Italian American experience beyond *Godfather* references, as evi-

denced by the time he comes back to the house with the more obscure, though nonetheless Sicilian, dessert, *zucotto*.

23. After the relative success of Savoca's first feature-length film, *True Love*, she obtained the help of some Hollywood heavyweights, including Jonathan Demme, who was an executive producer of *Household Saints*.

24. For example, she mocks her older son and daughter-in-law for giving their children "Anglo" names, asking, "Who will look over them, St. Scott and St. Stacy?"

25. Catherine's arranged marriage—prompted by a bet her father lost in a pinochle game—is at once a fantastical story steeped in local folklore and a sign of the patriarchal ways of her community.

CHAPTER FOUR

"All Colors, All Religions, All United"

Women Workers in California's Canneries

> No mass action is possible, if the masses in question are not convinced of the ends they wish to attain and the methods to be applied.
>
> —Antonio Gramsci, "The Southern Question"

In the above epigraph and elsewhere, Gramsci argues for the necessity of consciousness raising in any political or cultural transformation. To precipitate such a transformation—an alternative national popular culture—Gramsci posits the need for an organic intellectual, a thinker who can span the gap between the hegemonic culture and the counter-hegemonic. Likewise, he reminds us that a nuanced use of common sense, sprinkled, one might say, with good sense, can help deconstruct the ruling hegemony and thus promote cultural transformation. That is, he illustrates an understanding of the significance of one's everyday life in relation to the greater forces of a dominant national popular culture.

This chapter looks at the historical documentation and creative representation of cannery labor, mainly in and around San Diego, California, to explore the ways in which the relationship between women workers of different ethnicities and races can help us understand how local communities both sustain certain hegemonies and displace them with new counter-hegemonies; such displacement, I argue presently, may herald the development of a Gramscian national popular culture. Further, this chapter will examine representations of the experiences of cannery workers, most of whom were immigrant women, and suggest that the lives of such women ought to be considered crucial parts of larger national formations of ethnic identity and community building. In the case of Italian American cannery workers, this connection underscores the complex relationship Italian Americans have to assimilation and their sometimes-precarious position as white Americans.

The present focus is chiefly on cultural representation. Thus I examine photographs of cannery workers (one of the few forms of representations of cannery worker experience that exist in significant numbers) in an effort to assert the importance of such visual representations in any fully historical understanding of labor's role in the previous century; this understanding, in turn, can help bring to the surface an alternative national popular culture based on the lives of subaltern classes. More specifically, this chapter considers one man's efforts to illustrate visually the impact of women's work on the history of San Diego's various immigrant communities. Thomas Martinez, an eighty-two-year-old San Diego native, attempted (with different degrees of success) to reunite former cannery workers through the visual medium of a photograph. A discussion of what Martinez's efforts might suggest about the role of historical recuperation in the development of a new, national popular culture brings us to a more general survey of the diversity of the cannery workers' backgrounds. In particular, such a survey imagines the possibility of uncovering cross-ethnic or cross-racial alliances. Gramsci's views about the importance of everyday experiences in the name of creating a counter-hegemony, as well as his call for alliances between different subaltern classes, highlight the possibility of a national popular culture culled from visual representations, such as photographs. Along the way, I offer critical commentary on the development of ethnic identities in California as understood through the history of cannery labor and in relation to an overlooked Hollywood film, *Westward the Women*, directed by William Wellman.

While there are many historical questions that could be asked of an ethnically mixed group of cannery workers, the present goal is not to recuperate wholly cannery worker histories or California's history. Such projects are best left to historians. (Much valuable work with respect to canneries in California has been done by people such as Glenna Matthews, Carol Lynn McKibben, Patricia Zavella, Gloria Ricci Lothrop, Chris Friday, Vicki Ruiz, and Jaclyn Greenberg.) Cannery worker history, even in California alone, is long and intricate and varies dramatically according to city or region, time period, and type of cannery work—fish, vegetable, or fruit. Cannery worker history, within the discipline of labor history, has always had a marginal status, a consequence, most of the above-mentioned scholars argue, of the fact that the job itself was seasonal and, therefore, unsteady, and the majority of the workers were immigrant women with diverse backgrounds. Nevertheless, the history of cannery workers in California presents the cultural critic with an opportunity to think about the dynamics between ethnicity, race, class, and gender in America. It further permits us to repurpose Gramsci's theories for a location quite different from the rural Sardegna and urban Turin out of which they first developed. The work of people like Martinez points to possibilities for analysis and action—both with respect to historical recovery and contemporary political change—that are in line with Gramsci's ideas, albeit here with an emphasis on women's labor.

Photographic Memories

In 1998 and 1999 Thomas Martinez spearheaded a reunion of San Diego cannery workers. The canneries had been closed for years, but their history was well preserved in the memories of former workers and the community at large. Martinez, a San Diego native who never worked in a cannery but who had friends and family who did, organized, in great part by word of mouth, the first reunion of cannery workers in one of the city's largest Latino neighborhoods, Barrio Logan. According to *San Diego Union Tribune* coverage of the event, the majority of the former cannery workers present at that first gathering were Mexican Americans. In fact, the event's announcement, published in the *Tribune*, invoked only Latino workers:

> Former tuna cannery workers and their families will gather for a Labor Day celebration Monday at Crosby Park near downtown San Diego's waterfront. . . . the tuna canneries employed large numbers of women. Many were Hispanic, prompting labor leaders to coin the phrase "Rosita the Canner." (B-2, 5 September 1998)

Yet cannery workers were not just Latinas, something Martinez also knew. Martinez later stated that while the Labor Day event had been organized mainly with the Mexican American community in mind, he hoped to see the event grow to include all the former cannery workers.[1] And barely a month later, on Columbus Day, Martinez took a black-and-white 1930s-era cannery worker photograph to San Diego's India Street—the core of the city's Italian American neighborhood and the site of the yearly Columbus Day Festival. (The irony, to put it quite lightly, that such a sign of solidarity from the Latino community occurred on Columbus Day—a day that, depending on one's perspective, celebrates immigrant success stories or indigenous genocide—should not be overlooked.)

The heyday for San Diego's Italian neighborhood came prior to the completion in 1962 of Highway 5, a construction project that prompted many families to move out of the neighborhood, in what was a common postwar move to the suburbs as Italian Americans assimilated into the white cultural/racial landscape.² The slow demise of the fishing industry, the economic lifeblood of the Italian community, had led many to leave even before the construction of the freeway.³ Yet for such holidays as Columbus Day, San Diego Italian Americans return in no small number to what remains of the old neighborhood.

Today, India Street's residents are mostly working-class Mexican Americans, although most of the commerce surrounding the residential neighborhood has a distinct Italian flavor and is indeed owned by Italian Americans. As Verdicchio explains, "Though the area is no longer predominantly inhabited by Italians the tenor of life along its streets is still conditioned by that past presence and by the current thriving Italian food shops, restaurants and cafes" ("The Place of Identity" 15). Many of the Italian businesses announce themselves with nostalgic and symbolic images of an Italy long gone: Italian peasant dresses and aprons perpetually hanging to dry on a clothes line in the middle of one restaurant's garden area perhaps sum up best India Street's current style. This style resonates with the basic tone of the Columbus Day street fair—Sinatra, grilled sausages, and Italian flags in abundance.

Martinez found himself in this cultural mélange—sandwiched between the booth for the India Street reconstruction project and a restaurant selling *calamari fritti*. His was an understated booth with an old black-and-white photograph displayed on its table. The four-foot-long, 1930s-era photograph depicted the tuna cannery workers—the majority of whom were women—of San Diego Packing (later Bumble Bee Seafoods) clustered together in neat rows, as if posing for a class picture. It was a picture like many others, and yet one that was particularly important to a community that used to rely solely on the fishing industry for subsistence and economic mobility. The photograph became Martinez's madeleine, his attempt to awaken a certain memory in San Diegans. His goal, though, was not a nostalgic journey into the city's past but a mass recognition of cross-ethnic alliances (albeit only work related) and acknowledgment of the importance of cannery labor to the city's history and development.

Cannery Workers: Reimagining a Multicultural History

The photograph Martinez used in his reunion efforts illustrates much of what is known about the identity of San Diego seafood cannery workers—most of the workers in the photograph, like most of the cannery workers in town, were women. Moreover, their names, which had been written out on the back of the photograph, suggest that most of them had immigrant roots—they came from Italian, Mexican, Portuguese, and Japanese families (and, indeed, the San Diego cannery workers were drawn mainly from these four groups).

Throughout California the canning industry had provided work for many immigrants, including Italian Americans. Work in the canneries was seasonal and relied heavily on women, who were hired to do most of the cutting, cleaning, packing, and labeling of canned fish, meats, fruits, and vegetables. The majority of cannery workers, supervisors excluded, were women, and large numbers of Italian American women worked in California canneries from the late nineteenth century until the 1950s, and even into the decades that followed. As Martinez's project illustrates, cannery workers were by no means only from Italian backgrounds, but it is unclear whether this diverse workforce shared experiences beyond the cannery floors.

Martinez's grassroots effort to recognize a history of first- and second-generation American women workers in San Diego underscores the kind of reimagining of history that is at the heart of my project's historical readings of women at work within Italy and the United States. His attempt at forming a cross-cultural recognition of women's labor within San Diego suggests how alliances between different immigrant communities could help the social structure of contemporary San Diego. Martinez's actions are, self-consciously or not, essentially Gramscian. His emphasis of the need for alliances and his desire to recall the past in relation to the everyday lives of working migrant women place him in a position of a kind of organic intellectual. Using photography, a visual medium, is a plausible extension of the consciousness-raising language Gramsci called for in organizing subaltern classes. Photography literally becomes the language by which Martinez attempts to bring people to a new level of understanding about their own labor histories and class experiences.

His effort to use a street fair to preserve the history of gendered labor suggests an unconventional way to approach the subjects of race, women, and, especially relevant to my present study, Italian American history. The discovery of such hidden and fragile histories leads us to question if there were alliances between different immigrant communities, and if so, what they looked like. What happened to the various communities' ethnic identities? In what ways did intergroup solidarity respond to, increase, or diminish assimilationist pressures? That is, Martinez's not-unqualifiedly successful efforts at getting Italian American women interested in his project might suggest that as Italian Americans moved en masse toward a somewhat stable position of whiteness, they detached themselves from any past alliances they may have had with other immigrant or nondominant classes. The fact that memory, or "the loss of . . . memory," as Jennifer Guglielmo puts it, plays a part in Martinez's organizing efforts lends support to the argument that certain ethnic groups at times shed their immigrant—and nonwhite—status by consciously (or not) forgetting that nonwhite position (1).[4]

David Roediger, in his *Wages of Whiteness*, examines how the U.S. white working class began articulating its whiteness as a "wage," which it used to its benefit as a way to distinguish itself from other minority groups. He initiates his discussion by documenting, as others have before him, the gaps in labor histories' discussions of race. He suggests that we can create a more nuanced study of race and working-class histories if we move beyond only studying evidence from "political leaders, intellectuals" and "trade union practices," and emphasize instead cultural manifestations of working-class communities (110). Roediger is asking for a Gramscian-style focus on a broad-based vernacular culture. Martinez's undertaking and, in effect, the large black-and-white photograph he carried with him were signs of this effort. The use of a photograph to jar a community's memory, to remind it, perhaps, of the "common sense" aspects of its own histories, shows how cultural texts are tied up in how a community thinks of itself and how others see it. Representation of a certain kind of reality, in this case through a photograph (but similarly possible through a novel, film, or song), comes to illustrate how Italian Americans' memory loss, forgetting their past as workers, is linked to their privileging of a certain hegemonic cultural position.

Because the historical record of cannery workers is so limited, work done by grassroots intellectuals like Martinez is that much more important. It also reminds us of the usefulness of seeing the less visible forms of culture and resistance that Gramsci encourages us to notice. That is, negotiating the kind of studies of labor that Roediger calls for becomes challenging in the case of cannery workers, because the majority of textual sources on the subject of canneries focus on information about large-scale organizing efforts, cannery workers' legal relationships with fishermen's unions, and the details of how mechanization changed (and ultimately deteriorated) cannery work.[5] Thus looking for lesser-known or hidden forms of culture becomes essential.

In 1999, the Second Cannery Worker Reunion was held in San Diego on Labor Day. Martinez said the party was once again a success, even though it was only attended by members of the Mexican American community. According to Martinez, while relatively few people stopped to look at his picture booth on Columbus Day the prior year, those who did were curious and intrigued by his project. He also explained, with excitement, that "a good number" of Italian American women, many former cannery workers, had approached his booth. They were thrilled to see the photograph and to talk about the canneries, but most told Martinez that they would not come to a cannery worker reunion held in downtown San Diego, only a few minutes away from where they were standing with him on India Street. Many live in suburban San Diego now, and while they had made the trip to the city for Columbus Day, few were interested in doing so for a cannery worker reunion. Martinez was not taken aback: Most of the women were old and, as he put it, "It's a long drive." Neither was he discouraged, and had already planned a meeting with Portuguese American and Japanese American organizations to talk to them about his reunion. Then he added, Columbus Day was just around the corner, and "I'll be there again with my picture."[6]

Immigration, Canneries, and California History Revisited

In William Wellman's 1951 film *Westward the Women*, Italian immigrant characters become white against the landscape of an evolving California, and in so doing the film offers a simplistic narrative of formation to demonstrate Italian American assimilation, one that the history of cannery workers and Martinez's project disrupts. The film's story, written by Italian-born Frank Capra (arguably the only film he worked on with explicitly Italian American characters), offers a somewhat ahistorical view of California's growth. It presents a fictional account of about 140 women pioneers who travel from Chicago to California in 1851 as mail-order brides for men who have been living in a desolate valley since the Gold Rush began.

The women are all of indeterminate European descent, except for an Irish, a French, and an Italian woman. The only other explicitly foreign-born person in the wagon train is the group's cook, a Japanese man, Ito. The foreign-born characters each speak their native language at some point, but the Italian woman, Signora Moroni, speaks no English. Along the trip, each foreign-born character in turn clashes with the group as a whole. When they arrive in California, the women are paired off with the men, and Signora Moroni, with an orange she has picked from a nearby tree in hand, marries the only Italian man in town. The Italian couple, from Genoa and Milan (nicely disturbing a long-standing misconception that all Italians in the United States come from southern Italy or Sicily), speak in an unsubtitled Italian of California's fruit trees and how happy they will be in their new country.[7] As they speak, their bodies are enveloped by dancing couples around them. Soon after, the Italian couple take their place in line to be married before a justice of the peace; the camera pulls back to reveal Ito standing alone. By the film's conclusion, everyone, it would seem, has a clearly delineated social position in California. The Italians are part of the group, assimilated yet unique in their shared language and love of fruit—they are, in fact, assimilated ethnic whites. Meanwhile, the Japanese immigrant remains detached and isolated from the heterosexual, white culture around him.

The film projects post–World War II attitudes about race and gender onto Gold Rush-era California; in so doing, it offers an instructive illustration of the operations of racialization in the United States and its effect on the creation and movement of communities. The use of fruit—California oranges in particular—is a reminder of the state's agricultural base, the main reason, in fact, for many immigrants' relocation to the state. Indeed, California's agricultural and fishing industries were particularly beneficial to many Italian immigrants, who quickly found work in those sectors—including, of course, in the canneries.[8] That in the 1850s, the time period within the film, oranges were not actually part of the landscape of California means little: For the film's contemporary viewers, though, California would have been equated with fruit orchards and the like. According to Jay Mechling's history of the orange, "Oranges," while oranges entered California with the Franciscan missionaries in the mid-eighteenth century, they only became a marketable fruit with the completion of the Southern Pacific Railroad in 1873. The film, though, uses oranges and all fruit as regional and ethnic markers—ones that cleverly bring together California and Italy.

The complexities of race, gender, and community among California's disparate immigrant populations sketched in Wellman's film are in fact at the heart of the history of the state's canning operations. A similar mix of American nativism and immigrant favoritism seemed to exist among cannery workers and owners. For example, in her study of cannery workers in the Santa Clara Valley, Jaclyn Greenberg shows that through the early part of the twentieth century, many Italian cannery workers made and saved enough capital to open their own canneries and that, for the most part, they only hired other Italian immigrants. (Her study to a certain extent accounts for the kind of indifference with which Martinez's reunion efforts were met.) Likewise, she explains that when the canneries employed workers from various ethnic groups, each group tended to stay to itself. Not only did Italians and other ethnic groups not get along, but "native born Americans from Europe" did not want to work with any immigrant group (133). She cites a 1917 report from the Industrial Welfare Commission that held that "Americans, that is Americanized Europeans, usually dislike working with Southern Europeans and especially with Asiatics [sic]" (133). Accordingly, U.S.-born Italian workers and owners on many occasions allied themselves more with northern Europeans than with the Portuguese, Mexican, Japanese, or Filipino workers. Greenberg refers to two labor actions in 1917 (in Santa Clara and Fresno) in which Mexican and Japanese workers joined together, on the one hand, and Italians and Germans, on the other (196). Greenberg goes on to explain that "With such differences separating workers one might assume that the resultant lack of solidarity among workers might prevent them from asserting their rights as workers" (134). However, she notes that "women turned their distinctions to their own advantages" and, in what would seem to be an anti-Gramscian action, found individual reasons to insist on improving work conditions (134). Greenberg's study of the cannery labor up until World War I implies a culturally divided labor force where each group looked out for itself and only came together with other groups when it was most expedient.

Yet we can perhaps see a more unifying tendency in organizing efforts, efforts that undertook to use the women's shared position as workers as a way to draw them together. In labor pamphlets, press releases, and newspaper articles, organizers again and again called for unity among all races and religions. For example, in the early 1950s the Distributive, Processing, and Office Workers of America, a New York–based union, undertook an ultimately failed attempt at uniting cannery workers in California. Included in the pamphlets they handed out to workers was a section called "All Colors, All Religions, All United," where they triumphantly state: "There is no room for racial or religious prejudices amongst us. Negroes, Jews, Puerto Ricans, Italians—all sorts of minority groups are in our midst" ([sic], Labor Archive, cannery ephemera file). How effective these calls for solidarity were in uniting diverse communities is unclear (but efforts such as Thomas Martinez's might help here). While the Office Workers of America's campaign to unionize cannery workers seems largely to have failed, other such attempts had more success, though working conditions only somewhat improved. Accordingly it seems that organizers had more luck getting workers to create alliances when it benefited workers directly (suggesting certain pitfalls to such efforts). Beginning in 1930, the Cannery and Agricultural Workers Industrial Union began organizing efforts, and in 1935 it "dis-established itself in favor of the Congress of Industrial Organizations (the CIO)," which was then forming (Starr 67). By the late 1930s another union, the American Federation of Labor (AFL) Cannery Workers Unions, representing 60,000 workers, mainly in Northern California and the Central Valley, successfully lobbied for a restricted ten-hour work day, with Sundays off (twelve-hour days were acceptable with particularly perishable products).[9]

These 1930s efforts to organize cannery workers and improve their working conditions recognized (in a Marxist fashion) the importance of uniting workers as laborers and not as separate immigrant groups, placing class solidarity above everything else. They point to approaches that seem to echo Gramsci's call for cross-community solidarity, an echo suggestive of the possibilities for political and social transformation from a diverse workforce. For example, in a 1938 CIO-led union, rally speeches were given first in English, then Italian, and finally in Spanish (April, *People's World*).[10] Such efforts to embrace all communities in attendance underscore how issues of diversity were part of organizing efforts and suggest that cross-ethnic solidarities were regarded as feasible. However, the persistence of ethnic tensions throughout cannery history illustrates that shared aims (e.g., improving working conditions) cannot always prevail over the power of specific cultures (a complication Gramsci would not have been quick to acknowledge). However, as Kevin Starr points out in passing, "ethnic rivalries divided the whites, who called themselves Americans, from their Portuguese, Italian, and Mexican counterparts" (69). Such divisions show that discrimination more often than not might be a function of economic privilege, as Roediger, among others, reminds us. That Italians at times were either in the position of immigrant or the position of non-hyphenated American suggests something about the pull of assimilation and the process of racialization; likewise it establishes that historical narratives about cannery labor are neither singular nor simple.

As a result, the main primary sources of information on cannery labor—newspapers, union pamphlets, legal documents, testimonials, and photographs—while somewhat limiting (as mentioned above) can lead to a history that shows a group of workers that were at sometimes-overlapping moments both culturally divided and unified. It is a complex history, one that is difficult to recount through any single text. The San Diego Historical Society's Photography Archive, as with other archival sources, houses dozens of photographs, such as the one Martinez displayed on Columbus Day, that document female immigrant labor at the canneries.[11] Although most of the photographs have only a few written descriptions (names and dates, mainly), they remain visual images that trace historical periods of a city and of a now-defunct workforce. Interestingly, while the photographs and Thomas Martinez's efforts establish the multiple ethnic and national identities of the cannery workers, many secondary sources about cannery workers focus, for good reason, on single communities within specific regions—the Chicano community of San Diego, the Filipino community of Monterrey, or the Italian community of San Francisco, for example.[12] These assertions of community identity make sense in that they promote the recording of detail-specific narratives about a group's historical presence and participation in community building. These projects are crucial to our understanding of labor history and the solidification of race and ethnicity as theoretical categories in the United States. Yet, as suggested earlier, within all kinds of textual representations one finds few records of cross-racial or cross-cultural histories. Except for an occasional mention there is no unified history of cannery work.

These historical fissures make it easy to overlook the fact that the cannery workers were always a multiracial, multicultural labor force. Cross-cultural histories and projects can illuminate relationships between workers of different races and ethnicities—they might suggest when, where, and why alliances were formed, and help imagine Gramsci's possibilities of alliance formation in action. Recognizing that cannery workers were not isolated ethnic groups promotes an understanding of local cultures as mutually conceived and built rather than constructed in isolation. Put yet another way, cross-cultural historical views of cannery workers demonstrate the potential (or lack thereof) of alliances in the creation of cultures and communities with or against those upheld by the nation-state (i.e., hegemonic or counter-hegemonic).

Martinez's cannery worker reunion efforts open up, then, the possibility for understanding the past outside of standard notions of representation and suggest ways to acknowledge women's labor as an integral part of the culture of community. Feminist labor historians have continued to recognize that the labor of women is decidedly absent, ignored, and/or distorted in conventional forms of historical documentation (history books, visual art, literature, etc.). Only through taking up varied textual examples can we hope to understand more completely the nuances of the production of culture with respect to the labor of migrant women. Gramsci, as has been repeatedly stated throughout this book, offers a useful way to extend our understanding of culture because of his emphasis on everyday experiences, folklore, and the role of subalterns and organic intellectuals and the relationships they have to the development of an alternative national popular culture. As Roediger also claims, by examining the differences in the creation of culture and recognizing that culture can have varying meanings, we can, paradoxically, recreate a more cohesive vision of the past.

Notes

1. Unless otherwise stated, all information and quotations from Martinez come from personal interviews.

2. On San Diego's Italian American community, see Pasquale Verdicchio's "The Place of Identity: San Diego's Little Italy and Community as Archive" and Teresa

Fiore's "Frances Stephenson's *Promises*, a Woman's *Bildungsroman*: Contradictions in Growing Up Female and Italian in San Diego."

3. See Lorenzo Madalena's 1959 novel *Confetti for Gino* for a vivid depiction of the pre–Highway 5 neighborhood and fishing industry as seen through the eyes of a young, second-generation Italian American man. Stephenson's unpublished novel, *Promises*, offers instead a female perspective of San Diego's Italian American community and fishing industry, focusing on the post–World War II era.

4. See chapter three for a discussion of Micaela Di Leonardo's rhetoric of nostalgia concept as applied to the issue of Italian American racial positionality.

5. Archival research for this chapter was conducted primarily in the San Francisco Public Library's Italian American collection, the Labor Archive at San Francisco State University, the Oakland Public Library's History Room, the San Diego Public Library's History Room, and the special collections of the Universities of California at San Diego and Berkeley.

6. As of this writing there were no more known cannery reunions after 1999. However, the city of San Diego is working on a much-debated public monument to the cannery workers, "The Cannery Workers Tribute."

7. The couple's provenance squares with the actual history of California's Italian immigrants, the majority of whom came from northern Italy. Sicilian fishing families, especially those that settled in southern California, were also common, but the Italian north was, popular misunderstandings aside, the source of most of California's Italians. On the other hand, the film's imputation of a sense of nationalist pride to its Italian characters represents an unfortunate anachronism as Italy was not a unified country in 1851.

8. One of the more famous such immigrants is probably Mark J. Fontana. He emigrated from Italy in 1867 and worked in the produce trade, helping to form the California Fruit Canners Association (1899) and the California Packing Corporation (1916)—the latter eventually became Del Monte Cannery. That Italian immigrants reached such levels of economic success suggests some of the ways they were seen as part of the dominant culture.

9. The AFL Cannery Workers Unions represented some of the workers in the counties of San Francisco, Alameda, Santa Clara, Sacramento, Solano, Yuba, and Sutter.

10. Similar multilanguage efforts were made by the AFL Cannery Workers Unions; in particular, see the San Francisco State University Labor Archive cannery ephemera file.

11. While occasionally reprinted in history books or for community projects, these photos are generally only viewed publicly in various San Diego restaurants and hotels. In fact, one San Diego native told me of looking up from her plate of grilled fish at an India Street restaurant and noticing a framed black-and-white photograph she had never seen before showing her mother and aunts cleaning tuna. Although the labor of women is being made visible by such displays, the photos when used as

ornaments are void of historical specificity and become aesthetic objects that add "Old World charm" to an establishment.

12. See, for instance, Ruiz's account of Mexican women cannery workers or Elizabeth Reis's article on Bay Area Italian American nonfish cannery workers (in Sensi-Isolani and Martinelli).

EPILOGUE

After Modotti

In 1932, the photographer and essayist Tina Modotti published a German-language pamphlet, *5,000,000 Widows, 10,000,000 Orphans, Women! Do You Want That Again?* imploring working women throughout the world to stop an impending world war. Her work demonstrates one way the themes present in this book have been considered and theorized in the past (albeit along more dogmatic Marxist lines). In a sense, her life and work can be seen as having an affinity with those of some of the cultural figures introduced in this book (think Renata Viganò or Thomas Martinez, not to mention Antonio Gramsci himself). Modotti successfully integrated theory and practice in her life by combining political activism with her better-known work as a photographer. As Verdicchio explains: "Having become more and more involved in socialist causes, Modotti had begun to use her camera as a tool of activism, and with [Edward] Weston she traveled throughout Mexico exploring life outside the capital" (*Dear Vocio* 12). Modotti, an active Communist Party member, was born in Italy in 1896 and immigrated to California at seventeen, where she worked as a seamstress and as an actor in San Francisco and later in Los Angeles. She lived on and off in Mexico for about ten years and died unexpectedly in 1942. She used her photography as a political tool that reinforced her commitment to anti-Fascist and anti-capitalist movements in Europe and North America. In particular, many of her photos document the poverty, exploitation, and struggles of Mexico's indigenous people.

In the antiwar article, Modotti invites her readers to join the Soviet cause, explaining—in a phrase that seems at once hilariously inappropriate given Modotti's feminism and sadly naïve given the Stalinist terror then underway—how the U.S.S.R. "is the fatherland of all workers" (2). She links women from all parts of the globe ("imperialist and colonialist countries everywhere") by juxtaposing specific worker struggles and protests in different locations, such as Poland, Indochina, and the United States (18). She then creates a de facto alliance between all women by naming them as "mothers, sisters, and workers" who together can "tear down barriers of racial hatred [and] chauvinism [that] the church and the ruling class retains and even expands . . ." (4). In addition, she argues that women and their labor are a necessary part of any cultural or political movement. She reminds women that they are central participants in their societies: "You, working women, must not forget that there can be no mass movement, no successful revolution, if you do not participate to the fullest possible extent" (19). Her argument affirms the kind of alliance formation and recognition of multileveled experiences Gramsci outlines in his writings. Yet she expands on Gramsci's model by explicitly noting the deep impact of women's participation in any class-based revolution. Highlighting the need for women to recognize their potential to effect change, she ends her piece by reminding women that "each of your actions—at home, at work, on the street—must be a class conscious proletarian action" (19). In such a way she recognizes everyday forms of resistance, and she reminds us of the relationship between the private domestic space and the public market space, insisting all the while on the importance of being aware of one's position in relation to dominant hegemonic forces. However great the failures of the major Communist experiments in twentieth-century government, socialist ideals such as those embraced by Modotti remain provocative and, moreover, suggest possible directions for theorizing on the subject of women, migration, and labor.

The aim throughout this book has been to take into account how and when representations of migrant women's labor shape culture and perhaps provoke political and cultural changes (inasmuch as these are separate). Gramsci's thoughts on culture are useful to such a consideration of women, labor, and migration. As Verdicchio explains with respect to Gramsci's essay *The Southern Question*, "Gramsci's concepts . . . provide powerful insights into the potential construction of alternative circuits of knowledge and culture" (*Bound by Distance* 4). Most relevant to my project has been Gramsci's elaboration of the idea of national popular culture, particularly when considered alongside his insistence on the need for culture building through alliances between different subaltern classes and organic intellectuals and through a recognition of the significance of folklore (congruent with "common sense") and everyday experiences.

The everyday attempt at alliance-formation and historical recovery of immigrant women's labor discussed in chapter four's analysis of Thomas Martinez's actions suggest one practical and contemporary application of many of the theoretical and historical moves made throughout this book. As with the cannery worker example, many of the cultural sites discussed lie beyond the conventional bounds of historical or aesthetic narratives—for example, rice worker songs, contemporary immigrant testimonials, and independent U.S. cinema. My critical readings demonstrate how migrant women's labor and the representation of that labor is connected to the production of culture—from everyday habits and traditions, such as cooking, to exceptional political responses, such as anti-Fascist resistance. Moreover, my readings show varying ways in which labor and its textual sites create, sustain, and at times disrupt the hegemony of a nation-state.

Further, such less widely examined representations of women at work (as those examined here—cannery work in California, rice work in Italy, and domestic work in the United States and Italy) implicitly demand for explicit discussions of the construction of race and identity. In other words, serious considerations of the history and culture of a nation-state should always be complicated by the intersections of gender, race, class, and ethnicity. Such considerations by definition veer away from isolationist readings of culture and force a sometimes more difficult but always more rewarding recognition of the multifaceted systems of power, control, and agency. A look at Gramsci's theories with an emphasis on feminism and migration can only further such a process, as Gramsci encourages us to look beyond the obvious. In short, he reminds us that the lives of subaltern classes (such as migrant women) are inherently connected to struggles for hegemony.

The textual and cultural sites addressed in these pages resonate in sometimes extremely different ways with Modotti's efforts to unite women workers. That photography plays a prominent role in Modotti's project suggests an important way cultural representation can be used as a medium for expressing more abstract philosophical positions as well the complexities of the formation of identity within a national and global landscape. Our shared emphases on representation indicates a certain continuity, however coincidental, between our efforts—a continuity that gestures toward a political alternative that projects such as the present one can, I hope, help promote.

Bibliography

Absalom, Roger. *Italy Since 1800: A Nation in the Balance?* London: Longman, 1995.
Albers, Patricia, Exhibition Curator. *Dear Vocio: Photographs by Tina Modotti.* La Jolla, CA: University Art Gallery, 1997.
Alberti, Margherita Di Fazio. *Il servo nella narrativa italiana della prima metà dell'Ottocento.* Napoli: Liguori Editore, 1982.
Allen, Beverly and Mary Russo, Eds. *Revisioning Italy: National Identity and Global Culture.* Minneapolis, MN: University of Minnesota Press, 1997.
Ancona, Giovanni. "Labour Demand and Immigration in Italy." *Journal of Regional Policy* 11 (1991): 143–148.
Andall, Jacqueline. "Women Migrant Workers in Italy." *Women's Studies International Forum* 15.1 (1992): 41–48.
Anderson, Benedict. *Imagined Communities: Reflections on the Origin and Spread of Nationalism.* London: Verso, 1991.
Arbizzani, Luigi. "Le lavoratrici delle campagne durante il fascismo e la Resistenza nella Valle Padana." *Istituto Alcide Cervi Annali* 13 (1991): 223–246.
Aricò, Santo L., Ed. *Contemporary Women Writers in Italy: A Modern Renaissance.* Amherst, MA: University of Massachusetts Press, 1990.
Baker, Aaron and Julian Vitullo. "Mysticism and the *Household Saints* of Everyday Life." *Voices in Italian Americana* 7.2 (1996): 55–68.
Bakhtin, Mikhail M. *The Dialogic Imagination.* Ed. Michael Holquist. Austin, TX: University of Texas Press, 1981.
———. *Speech Genres and Other Late Essays.* Trans. Vern W. McGee. Austin, TX: University of Texas Press, 1994.
Barbieri, Remigo. "Mondine di Medicina." *Donne emiliane nella Resistenza, Terzo Quaderno di 'La Lotta.'* Bologna: Arte e Stampa, 1964, 47–50.

Barolini, Helen, Ed. *The Dream Book: An Anthology of Writings by Italian American Women*. Syracuse, NY: Syracuse University Press, 2001.
———. *Umbertina*. New York: The Feminist Press, 1998.
Baron, Ava, Ed. *Work Engendered: Toward a New History of American Labor*. Ithaca, NY: Cornell University Press, 1991.
Bartocci, Enzo and Vittorio Cotesta, Eds. *L'identità italiana: Emigrazione, immigrazione, conflitti etnici*. Quaderni della Fondazione Giacomo Brodolini. Rome: Lavoro, 1999.
Belluci, Stefano and Sante Matteo, Eds. *Africa Italia: Due continenti si avvicinano*. Santarcangelo di Romagna, Italy: Fara, 1999.
Bendotti, Angelo and Eugenia Valtulina, Eds. *Il pane degli altri: Emigrati ed immigrati nella provincia di Bergamo dalla fine dell'Ottocento ai giorni nostri*. Bergamo: Il filo di Arianna, 1995.
Bengiveno, Teri Ann, Laura Ruberto, and Kathleen L. Rogers. "CON LE NOSTRE MANI: Italian Americans at Work in the East Bay." *Italian Immigrants Go West: The Impact of Locale on Ethnicity*. Eds. Janet E. Worrall, Carol Bonomo Albright, and Elvira G. Di Fabio. Cambridge, MA: American Italian Historical Association, 2003, 1–9.
Benjamin, Walter. "Theses on the Philosophy of History." *Illuminations*. Trans. Harry Zohn. New York: Random House, 1985, 253–264.
Berlanstein, Leonard R. *Rethinking Labor History*. Urbana, IL: University of Illinois Press, 1993.
Bevilacqua, Piero, Andreina De Clementi, and Emilio Franzina, Eds. *Storia dell'emigrazione Italiana*. Rome: Donzelli Editore, 2001.
Biasin, Gian Paolo. "Gelato e peperoncino." *Forum Italicum* 29.1 (1995): 103–113.
Birnbaum, Lucia Chiavola. *Liberazione della donna: Feminism in Italy*. Middletown, CT: Wesleyan University Press, 1986.
Bona, Mary Jo. *Claiming a Tradition: Italian/American Women Writers*. Bloomington, IL: Southern Illinois University Press, 1999.
———, Ed. *The Voices We Carry*. Montreal: Guernica, 1994.
Bondanella, Peter. *Italian Cinema: From Neorealism to the Present*. 1983. New York: Continuum Press, 1991.
Bono, Paolo and Sandra Kemp, Eds. *Italian Feminist Thought: A Reader*. Oxford: Basil Blackwell, 1991.
Bortdotti, Franca Pieroni. *Socialismo e questione femminile in Italia. 1892–1922*. Milan Mazzitta, 1974.
Bouchane, Mohamed. *Chiamatemi Alì*. Eds. Carla De Girolamo and Daniele Miccione. Milan: Leonardo Editore, 1990.
Braidotti, Rosi. *Nomadic Subjects: Embodiment and Sexual Difference in Contemporary Feminist Theory*. New York: Columbus University Press, 1994.
Braybon, Gail and Penny Summerfield. *Out of the Cage: Women's Experiences in Two World Wars*. London: Pandora Press, 1987.
Brodkin, Karen. *How Jews Became White Folks and What That Says about Race in America*. New Brunswick, NJ: Rutgers University Press, 1998.

Brunetta, Gian Piero. *Cent'anni di cinema italiano: Volume 2 dal 1945 ai giorni nostri.* Rome: Editori Laterza, 1995.

Bruno, Giuliana. *Streetwalking on a Ruined Map: Cultural Theory and the City Films of Elvira Notari.* Princeton, NJ: Princeton University Press, 1993.

Bruno, Giuliana and Maria Nadotti, Eds. *Off Screen: Women and Film in Italy.* London: Routledge, 1988.

Burns, Jennifer. "Exile within Italy: Interactions between Past and 'Homes' in Texts in Italian by Migrant Writers." *Annali d'Italianistica* 20 (2002): 369–384.

Cabrini, A. *Alle risaiole: Discorso pronunciato dal Deputato A. Cabrini al parlamento nazionale.* Camera del lavoro di Reggio Emilia, 1903.

Calhoun, Craig, Ed. *Habermas and the Public Sphere.* Cambridge, MA: MIT Press, 1992.

Camarca, Claudio. *Migranti: Verso una terra chiamata Italia.* Milan: Rizzoli, 2003.

Candelora, Giorgio. *Storia dell'Italia moderna.* Vols. 1–11. 1984. Milan: Feltrinelli, 1993.

"Cannery Worker Reunion Announcement." Author unknown. *San Diego Union Tribune*, September 5, 1998, B–2.

Carby, Hazel. *Reconstructing Womanhood: The Emergence of the Afro-American Woman Novelist.* New York: Oxford University Press, 1987.

Carlini, Giuliano, Ed. *La terra in faccia: Gli immigrati raccontano.* Rome: Ediesse, 1991.

Carson, Diane, Linda Dittmar, and Janice R. Welsch, Eds. *Multiple Voices in Feminist Film Criticism.* Minneapolis, MN: University of Minnesota Press, 1994.

Castellani, Giuliana. Untitled talk "L'Emigrazione al femminile: Atti del Convegno, Bologna 12–13 Gennaio 1990." *I flussi migratori dell'Emilia-Romagna*, no. 7. Bologna: Tipografia Compositori, 1990.

Chohra, Nassera with Alessandra Atti di Sarro. *Volevo diventare bianca.* Rome: Edizioni E/O, 1993.

Clialente, Fausta, "Viaggio in risaia," Noi donne, 1953.

Ciarnelli, Marcella, Miss Italia Correspondent. *L'Unità*, September 5–8, 1996.

Cigarini, Lia, Ed. *La Rivoluzione inatessa: Donne al mercato del lavoro.* Milano: Pratiche Editrice, 1997.

Ciongoli, Kenneth A. and Jay Parini, Eds. *Beyond The Godfather: Italian American Writers on the Real Italian American Experience.* Hanover, NH: University Press of New England, 1997.

Clark, Donald Martin. *States of Grace: Senegalese in Italy and the New European Immigration.* Minneapolis, MN: University of Minnesota Press, 1997.

Clark, Martin. *Modern Italy 1871–1995.* 2nd ed. London: Longman. 1995.

Clò, Clarissa and Teresa Fiore. "Unlikely Connections: Italy's Cultural Formations between Home and the Diaspora." *Diaspora: A Journal of Transnational Studies* 10.3 (2001): 415–441.

Cohen, Miriam. *Workshop to Office: Two Generations of Italian Women in New York City, 1900–1950.* Ithaca, NY: Cornell University Press, 1992.

Colombi, Marchesa. *In risaia: Racconto di natale.* 1878. Novara: Centro Novarese di Studi Letterari, 1994.

Colombo, Asher. "Hope and Despair: 'Deviant' Immigrants in Italy." *Journal of Modern Italian Studies* 2.31 (1997): 1–19.
Colombo, Asher and Giuseppe Sciortino, Eds. *Assimilati ed esclusi*. Bologna: Il Mulino, 2002.
———, Eds. *Un'immigrazione normale*. Bologna: Il Mulino, 2003.
Colombo, Enzo, Ed. *Matrimonio in brigata: Le opere e i giorni di Renata Viganò e Antonio Meluschi*. Bologna: Grafis, 1995.
Coluccia, Anna. *Immigrazione, nuove realtà e nuovi cittadini*. Politiche e servizi sociali. Milan: F. Angeli, 1998.
Cometto, Maria Teresa. *La Marchesa Colombi: La prima giornalista del "Corriere della Sera."* Turin: B.L.U. Editoriale, 1996.
Cornelisen, Ann. *Women of the Shadows: The Wives and Mothers of Southern Italy*. New York: Random House, 1977.
Coro delle mondine di Correggio. *Mondariso*. I Dischi del Mulo, the City of Correggio and Discoland, 1996.
Cortés, Carlos. E. "Italian-Americans in Film: From Immigrants to Icons." *Melus* 14.3–4 (1987): 107–126.
Crisantino, Amelia, Ed. *Ho trovato l'occidente: Storie di donne immigrate a Palermo*. Palermo: La Luna, 1992.
Curcio, Renato. *Shish Mahal*. Rome: Sensibili alle Foglie, 1991.
Davis, John A., Ed. *Gramsci and Italy's Passive Revolution*. London: Croom Helm, 1979.
De Grazia, Victoria. *How Fascism Ruled Women: Italy 1922–1945*. Berkeley: University of California Press, 1992.
de Lauretis, Teresa. *Technologies of Gender: Essays on Theory, Film and Fiction*. Bloomington, IN: Indiana University Press, 1987.
di Leonardo, Micaela. *The Varieties of Ethnic Experience: Kinship, Class, and Gender among California Italian-Americans*. Ithaca, NY: Cornell University Press, 1984.
Di Scala, Spencer M. *Italy: From Revolution to Republic, 1700 to the Present*. Boulder, CO: Westview Press, 1995.
Doane, Mary Ann. "Film and the Masquerade: Theorizing the Female Spectator." *Writing on the Body: Female Embodiment and Feminist Theory*. Eds. Katie Conboy, Nadia Medina, and Sarah Stanbury. New York: Columbia University Press, 1997, 176–194.
Ets, Marie Hall. *Rosa, the Life of an Italian Immigrant*. Madison, WI: University of Wisconsin Press, 1999.
Ewen, Elizabeth. *Immigrant Women in the Land of Dollars: Life and Culture on the Lower East Side, 1890–1925*. New York: Monthly Review Press, 1985.
Ferraro, Thomas J. "Blood in the Marketplace: The Business of Family in the Godfather Narratives." *The Invention of Ethnicity*. Ed. Werner Sollors. Oxford: Oxford University Press, 1989.
Fiore, Teresa. "Frances Stephenson's *Promises*, a Woman's *Bildungsroman*: Contradictions in Growing Up Female and Italian in San Diego." *Italian Immigrants Go West: The Impact of Locale on Ethnicity*. Eds. Janet E. Worrall, Carol Bonomo Albright,

and Elvira G. Di Fabio. Cambridge, MA: American Italian Historical Association, 2003, 25–37.

———. "Reconfiguring Urban Space as Thirdspace: The Case of Little Italy, San Diego (California)." *Adjusting Sites: New Essays in Italian American Studies*. Eds. William Boelhower and Rocco Pallone. Filibrary Series 16. 1999, 89–110.

———. "The Ship as a Pre-occupied Space: A Theoretical and Applied Approach to Migrant Culture between Italy and the United States." *Comparative Sites of Ethnicity: Europe and the Americas*. Eds. Carmen Birkle, William Boelhower, and Rocio Davis. Heidelberg: Winter Verlag, 2004, 29–44.

Fofi, Goffredo. Interview by Carlo Mazzacurati. *Linea D'Ombra*, 118 (1996): 13–16.

Fortunato, Mario and Salah Methnani. *Immigrato*. Rome: Theoria, 1990.

Fraser, Nancy. "Rethinking the Public Sphere: A Contribution to the Critique of Actually Existing Democracy." *Social Text* 8–9.25–26 (1990): 56–80.

Friday, Chris. *Organizing Asian American Labor: The Pacific Coast Canned Salmon Industry, 1870–1942*. Philadelphia: Temple University Press, 1995.

Friedman, Lester D., Ed. *Unspeakable Images: Ethnicity and the American Cinema*. Urbana, IL: University of Illinois Press, 1991.

Gabaccia, Donna R. *Italy's Many Diasporas*. London: Taylor and Francis, 2000.

Gabaccia, Donna R. and Franca Iacovetta, Eds. *Women, Gender, and Transnational Lives: Italian Workers of the World*. Toronto: University of Toronto Press, 2004.

Gabree, John. *Gangsters: From "Little Caesar" to "The Godfather."* New York City: Galahad Books, 1973.

Gagliani, Dianella, Elda Guerra, Laura Mariani, and Fiorenza Tarozzi. "Il racconto della Resistenza femminile: Tradizione e ricerca." Unpublished manuscript, 1997.

Gardaphè, Fred L. *From Wiseguys to Wise Men: The Gangster and Italian American Masculinities*. New York: Routledge, 2006.

———. *Leaving Little Italy: Essaying Italian American Culture*. Albany: State University of New York Press, 2004.

Gardiner, Michael. *The Dialogics of Critique: M. M. Bakhtin and the Theory of Ideology*. Routledge: London, 1992.

Gedaf, Irene. "Can Nomads Learn to Count to Four? Rosi Braidotti and the Space for Difference in Feminist Theory." *Women: A Cultural Review* 7.2 (1996): 189–202.

Gennari, John. "Passing for Italian: Crooners and Gangsters in Crossover Culture." *Transitions* 72.6.4 (1996): 36–72.

Ginzburg, Natalia. *Ti ho sposato per allegria e altre commedie*. Turin: Einaudi, 1968.

Giunta, Edvige. *Writing with an Accent: Contemporary Italian American Women Authors*. New York: Palgrave, 2002.

Gluck, Berger Sherna. *Rosie the Riveter Revisited: Women, the War and Social Change*. New York: Penguin, 1987.

Gnisci, Armando. "La letteratura dell'immigrazione." *Forum Italicum* 30.2 (1996).

Gramsci, Antonio. *An Antonio Gramsci Reader: Selected Writings: 1916–1935*. Ed. David Forgacs. New York: Schocken Books, 1988.

———. Gli intellectuali el'organizzazione della cultura. 1975. Rome: Riuniti, 1996.
———. Lettere dal carcere. Ed. Paolo Spriano. 1947. Turin: Einaudi, 1971.
———. I Quaderni: Letteratura e vita nazionale. 1975. Rome: Riuniti, 1996.
———. I Quaderni: Note sul Machiavelli sulla politica e sullo stato moderno. 1975. Rome: Riuniti, 1996.
———. The Southern Question. Trans. and introduction by Pasquale Verdicchio. West Lafayette, IN: Bordighera, 1995.
Green, Nancy L. *Ready-to-Wear and Ready-to-Work: A Century of Industry and Immigrants in Paris and New York*. Durham, NC: Duke University Press, 1997.
Greenberg, Jaclyn. *Industry in the Garden: A Social History of the Canning Industry and Cannery Workers in the Santa Clara Valley, California, 1870–1920*. Los Angeles: UCLA, 1985.
Grewal, Inderpal and Caren Kaplan, "Introduction: Transnational Feminist Practices and Questions of Postmodernity." *Scattered Hegemonies: Postmodernity and Transnational Feminist Practices*. Eds. Inderpal Grewal and Caren Kaplan. Minneapolis, MN: University of Minnesota Press, 1994, 1–35.
Gualandi, Irea. *Mondine tra cronaca, storia, e testimonianze*. Rome: Ediesse, 1984.
Guglielmo, Jennifer and Salvatore Salerno, Eds. *Are Italians White? How Race Is Made in America*. New York: Routledge, 2003.
Guglielmo, Thomas A. *White on Arrival: Italians, Race, Color, and Power in Chicago, 1890–1945*. New York: Oxford University Press, 2003.
Habermas, Jurgen. *The Structural Transformation of the Public Sphere: An Inquiry into a Category of Bourgeois Society*. Trans. Thomas Burger. 1962. Cambridge, MA: MIT Press: 1994.
Hale, Grace Elizabeth. *Making Whiteness: The Culture of Segregation in the South, 1890–1940*. New York: Vintage, 1999.
Hall, Stuart. "Cultural Identity and Cinematic Representation." *Exiles: Essays on Caribbean Cinema*. Ed. Mbye Cham. Africa World Press, 1992, 220–236.
———. "Gramsci's Relevance for the Study of Race and Ethnicity." *Journal of Communication Inquiry* 10.2 (1986): 34–56.
———. "The Question of Cultural Identity." *Modernity: An Introduction to Modern Society*. Cambridge, MA: Blackwell, 1996, 595–634.
Hardt, Michael and Antonio Negri. *Empire*. Boston: Harvard University Press, 2001.
Hay, James. *Popular Film Culture in Fascist Italy: The Passing of the Rex*. Bloomington, IN: Indiana University Press, 1987.
Higson, Andrew. "The Concept of National Cinema." *Screen* 30 (1989): 36–46.
Hirschkop, Ken and David Shepherd, Eds. *Bakhtin and Cultural Theory*. Manchester: Manchester University Press, 1989.
Holub, Renate. *Antonio Gramsci: Beyond Marxism and Postmodernism*. London: Routledge, 1992.
Ignatiev, Noel. *How the Irish Became White*. New York: Routledge, 1995.
Jacobson, Matthew Frye. *Whiteness of a Different Color: European Immigrants and the Alchemy of Race*. Cambridge, MA: Harvard University Press, 1998.

Kaplan, Caren. "The Politics of Location as Transnational Feminist Practice." *Scattered Hegemonies: Postmodernity and Transnational Feminist Practices*. Eds. Inderpal Grewal and Caren Kaplan. Minneapolis, MN: University of Minnesota Press, 1994, 137–152.

Kerber, Linda K. *Toward an Intellectual History of Women*. Chapel Hill: University of North Carolina Press, 1997.

Khouma, Pap. *Io, venditore di elefanti: Una vita per forza fra Dakar, Parigi e Milano*. Ed. Oreste Pivetta. Milan: Garzanti, 1990.

Kroha, Lucienne. *The Woman Writer in Late Nineteenth-Century Italy: Gender and the Formation of Literary Identity*. Lewiston, NY: Edwin Mellon Press, 1992.

Lajolo, Davide. *Quaranta giorni quaranta notti: Romanzo*. Milan: Casa Editrice Ceschina, 1955.

Lakhous, Amara. *Scontro di civiltà per un ascensore a piazza Vittorio*. Milan: Edizione E/O, 2006.

Landy, Marcia. *Film, Politics, and Gramsci*. Minneapolis: University of Minnesota Press, 1994.

Lazzaro-Weis, Carol. *From Margins to Mainstream: Feminism and Fictional Modes in Italian Women's Writing, 1968–1990*. Philadelphia: University of Pennsylvania Press, 1993.

Lawton, Benjamin. "Tarantella." Unpublished article, 1999.

Lizzani, Carlo. *Riso amaro: Un film diretto da Giuseppe De Santis*. Rome: Officina Edizioni, 1978.

Lonzi, Carla. *Sputiamo su Hegel: Le donna clitoridea e la donna vaginale e altri scritti*. Milan: Rivolta Femminile, 1974.

Lothrop, Gloria Ricci. "The Italians of Los Angeles." *Fulfilling the Promise of California: An Anthology of Essays on the Italian American Experience in California*. Eds. Andrew Rolle and Gloria Ricci Lothrop. Norman, OK: Arthur H. Clark, 2000.

Lourdeux, Lee. *Italian and Irish Filmmakers in America: Ford, Capra, Coppola, and Scorsese*. Philadelphia: Temple University Press, 1990.

Lowe, Lisa. *Immigrant Acts. On Asian American Cultural Politics*. Durham, NC: Duke University Press, 1996.

Lowe, Lisa and David Lloyd. "Introduction." *The Politics of Culture in the Shadow of Capital*. Eds. Lisa Lowe and David Lloyd. Durham, NC: Duke University Press 1997, 1–32.

Madalena, Lorenzo. *Confetti for Gino*. Garden City, NY: Doubleday and Company, 1959.

Mafai, Miriam. *Pane nero: Donne e vita quotidiana nella seconda guerra mondiale*. Le Scie. Milan: Arnoldo Mondadori, 1987.

Mangione, Jerre and Ben Morreale. *La storia: Five Centuries of the Italian American Experience*. New York: Harper Collins Publishers, 1993.

Marcus, Millicent. *Italian Film in the Light of Neorealism*. Princeton, NJ: Princeton University Press, 1986.

———. "Miss Mondina, Miss Sirena, Miss Farina: The Feminized Body-Politic from *Bitter Rice* to *La voce della luna*." *Romance Languages Annual* 4 (1992): 296–300.

Matthews, Glenna. *Silicon Valley, Women, and the California Dream: Gender, Class, and Opportunity in the Twentieth Century*. Stanford, CT: Stanford University Press, 2003.

McCurry, Dan C. *Cannery Captives: Women Workers in the Produce Processing Industry*. New York: Arno Press, 1975.

McKibben, Carol Lynn. *Beyond Cannery Row: Sicilian Women, Immigration, and Community in Monterey, California, 1915–1999*. Bloomington, IL: Illinois University Press, 2006.

Mechling, Jay. "Oranges." *Rooted in America: Foodlore of Popular Fruits and Vegetables*. Eds. David Scofield Wilson and Angus K. Gillespie Knoxville, TN: University of Tennessee Press, 1999, 120–141.

Melliti, Moshen. *Pantanella: Canto lungo la strada*. Rome: Edizione Lavoro, 1992.

Meyer, Donald. *Sex and Power: The Rise of Women in America, Russia, Sweden, and Italy*. Middleton, CT: Wesleyan University Press, 1987.

Miceli Jeffries, Giovanna, Ed. *Feminine Feminists: Cultural Practices in Italy*. Minneapolis: University of Minnesota Press, 1994.

Micheletti, P. A. and Saidou Moussa Ba. *La promessa di Hamadi*. Novara: De Agostini, 1991.

The Milan Women's Bookstore Collective. *Sexual Differences: A Theory of Social-Symbolic Practice*. Trans. Patricia Cicogna and Teresa de Lauretis. Bloomington: Indiana University Press, 1990.

Modotti, Tina. *5,000,000 Widows, 10,000,000 Orphans, Women! Do You Want That Again?* 1932. Trans. Elizabeth Bredeck. La Jolla, CA: Parenthesis Writing Series, 1996.

Mohanty, Chandra Talpade. "Under Western Eyes: Feminist Scholarship and Colonial Discourse." *Third World Women and the Politics of Feminism*. Eds. Chandra Talpade Mohanty, Ann Russo, and Lordes Torres. Bloomington: Bloomington University Press, 1991.

Morson, Gary Saul and Carly Emerson. *Mikhail Bakhtin: Creation of a Prosaics*. Stanford, CT: Stanford University Press, 1990.

Mulvey, Laura. *Visual and Other Pleasures*. Bloomington: Indiana University Press, 1989.

Murphy, Timothy. Unpublished conference paper, "Expanding the Area of Autonomy: Music, Culture, and Politics in the Italian Counter-Culture 1964–977." *Italian Effect Conference*, Sydney, Australia, September 2004.

Nardini, Gloria. "Is it *True Love?* or Not? Patterns of Ethnicity and Gender in Nancy Savoca." *Voices in Italian Americana* 2.1 (1991): 10–17.

Negri, Ada. *Opere scelte*. Eds. Elena Cazzulani and Gilberto Coletto. Lodi: Edizione Lodigraf, 1984.

Nelli, Humbert S. *From Immigrants to Ethnics: The Italian Americans*. Oxford: Oxford University Press, 1983.

Noce, Teresa. *Gioventú senza sole*. Rome: Edizioni Riuniti, 1973.

———. *Vivere in piedi*. Milan: Gabriele Mazzotta Editore, 1978.

Odencrantz, Louise. *Italian Women in Industry. A Study of Conditions in New York City.* New York: Arno Press, 1977.
Overbey, David, Ed. and Trans. *Springtime in Italy: A Reader on Neorealsim.* Hamden, CT: Archon Books, 1978.
Palazzi, Maura. *Donne sole: Storia dell'altra faccia dell'Italia tra antico regime e società contemporanea.* Milan: Bruno Mondadori, 1997.
Parati, Graziella. *Migration Italy: The Art of Talking Back in a Destination Culture.* Toronto: Toronto University Press, 2005.
———. Ed. *Mediterranean Crossroads: Migration Literature in Italy.* Rutherford, NJ: Fairleigh Dickinson University Press and London: Associated University Press, 1999.
———. "Looking through Non-Western Eyes: Immigrant Women's Autobiographical Narratives in Italian." *Writing New Identities: Gender, Nation, and Immigration in Contemporary Europe.* Eds. Gisela Brinker-Gabler and Sidonie Smith. Minneapolis: University of Minnesota Press, 1997.
Parreñas, Rhacel Salazar. *Servants of Globalization: Women, Migration and Domestic Work.* Stanford, CT: Stanford University Press, 2001.
Paterlini, Marco, Ed. *Quando saremo a Reggio Emilia: Risaia padane e mondine reggiane.* Correggio (Reggio Emilia): Technograf, 1987.
Paulesu, Mimma. *Le donne di casa Gramsci.* Quercioli: Editori Riuniti, 1991.
Pavese, Cesare. "Tra donne sole." *La bella estate e altri romanzi.* 1949. Milan: Oscar Mondadori, 1986.
Per te mondina. Publication of the CGIL. Catalog 34/4. Bologna: Library of the Istituto Gramsci, ca. 1949.
Petronius. *Ricettario della felicità.* Bologna: Casa Editrice Capitol, 1961.
Picarazzi, Teresa. "Il viaggio di Awa and Women Writing Culture." *Romance Languages Annual* 9 (1998): 305–311.
Polchi, Vladimiro. "Giovene, credente e telemaniaco: Ecco l'identikit dell'immigrato." *La Repubblica*, May 11, 2006, 33.
Pucci, Idanna. *The Trials of Maria Barbella: The True Story of a 19th-century Crime of Passion.* New York: Random House, 1997.
Puzo, Mario. *The Fortunate Pilgrim.* 1964. New York: Lancer Books, 1973.
———. *The Godfather.* New York: Fawcett, 1969.
Quasi, Annarella. "Le mondine delle risaie vercellesi." *Istituto Alcide Cervi Annali* 12 (1990): 165–180.
Reich, Jacqueline. "Nancy Savoca: An Appreciation" *Italian Americana* 13.1 (1995): 11–15.
Roediger, David R. *The Wages of Whiteness: Race and the Making of the American Working Class.* New York: Verso, 1991.
Romero, Mary. *Maid in the U.S.A.* New York: Routledge, 1992.
Ruberto, Laura. "La contadina si ribella: Gendered Resistance in *L'Agnese va a morire.*" *Romance Languages Annual* 9 (1998): 328–335.
———. "Immigrants Speak: Italian Literature from the Border." *Forum Italicum* 31.1 (1997): 127–144.

———. "Grains of Truth: Rice, Labor, and Cultural Identity." In *Our Own Voices: Multidisciplinary Perspectives on Italian and Italian American Women*. Ed. Elizabeth G. Messina. Florida Atlantic University, Boca Raton, FL: Bordighera Press, 2003.

———. "Where Did the Goodfellas Learn How to Cook? Gender, Labor, and the Italian American Experience." *Italian Americana: Cultural and Historical Review*, Summer 2003, 164–176.

Ruberto, Laura E. and Kristi M. Wilson, Eds. *Italian Neorealism and Global Cinema*. Detroit, MI: Wayne State University Press, 2007.

Ruiz, Vicki L. and Ellen Carol DuBois, Eds. *Unequal Sisters: A Multicultural Reader in U.S. Women's History*, 2nd ed. New York: Routledge, 1994.

Said, Edward. *Culture and Imperialism*. New York: Alfred A. Knopf, 1993.

Sasson, Anne Showstack. *Gramsci's Politics*, 2nd ed. Minneapolis: University of Minnesota Press, 1980.

Sarti, Raffaella. "Zita, serva, e santa. Un modello da imitare?" *Modelli di santità e modelli di comportamento*. Eds. Giulia Barone, Marina Caffiero, and Francesco Scorza Barcellona. Turin: Rosenberg and Sellier, 1994, 307–359.

Sautman, Francesca Canadé. "Women of the Shadows: Italian American Women, Ethnicity and Racism in American Cinema." *Differentia* 6/7 (1994): 219–246.

Scott, Joan Wallach. *Gender and the Politics of History*. New York: Columbia University Press, 1988.

Sensi-Isolani, Paola A. and Phylis Cancilla Martinelli, Eds. *Struggle and Success: An Anthology of the Italian Immigrant Experience in California*. New York: Center for Migration Studies, 1993.

Sitney, P. Adams. *Vital Crisis in Italian Cinema: Iconography, Stylistics, Politics*. Austin: University of Texas Press, 1995.

Smith, Dennis Mack. *Mussolini*. New York: Knopf, 1982.

Soja, Edward W. *Thirdspace: Journeys to Los Angeles and Other Real-and-Imagined Places*. Oxford: Blackwell Publishers, 1996.

Spackman, Barbara. "The Fascist Rhetoric of Virility." *Stanford Italian Review* 8.1–2 (1990): 81–101.

Starr, Kevin. *Endangered Dreams: The Great Depression in California*. New York: Oxford UP, 1996.

Steinberg, James. "Cannery Veterans Savor Memories." *San Diego Union Tribune*, September 8, 1998, B3+.

Tamburri, Anthony Julian, Paolo A. Giordano, and Fred L. Gardaphè. *From the Margin: Writings in Italian Americana*. West Lafayette, IN: Purdue Univesity Press, 1991.

Turrini, Olga. *Le casalinghe di riserva: Lavoratrici domestiche e famiglia borghese*. Rome: Coines Edizioni, 1977.

Valentini, Chiara. *Le donne fanno paura*. Milan: Il Saggiatore, 1997.

Verdicchio, Pasquale. *Bound by Distance: Rethinking Nationalism through the Italian Diaspora*. Rutherford, NJ: Fairleigh Dickinson University Press, 1997.

———. *Devils in Paradise: Writings on Post-Emigrant Cultures.* Toronto: Guernica, 1997.

———. "Introduction." Exhibition. *Dear Vocio: Photographs by Tina Modotti: November 8, 1996 through January 11, 1997.* San Diego: University Art Gallery, University of California, 1997.

———. "The Place of Identity: San Diego's Little Italy and Community as Archive." *Italian Immigrants Go West: The Impact of Locale on Ethnicity.* Eds. Janet E. Worrall, Carol Bonomo Albright, and Elvira G. Di Fabio. Cambridge, MA: American Italian Historical Association, 2003, 10–24.

———. "*Tarantella.*" Dir. Helen de Michiel. Film Review. *Lightzoo: Italian Film in Review*, 1998. members.tripod.com/~verdicchio/lightzoo (November 11, 1998).

Vettori, Giuseppe, Ed. *Canzoni italiane di protesta: 1794–1974.* Rome: Newton Compton Editore, 1974.

Viganò, Renata. *L'Agnese va a morire.* 1949. Turin: Einaudi, 1993.

———. *Matrimonio in brigata.* Milan: Vangelista, 1976.

———. *Una storia di ragazze.* Milan: Cino del Duca Editore, 1962.

———. *Ho conosciuto Ciro.* Bologna: Technografica Emiliana, 1959.

———. *Donne nella Resistenza.* Bologna: S.T.E.B., 1955.

———. *Arriva la cicogna.* [n.p.]: Edizioni di Cultura Sociale, 1954.

———. *Le mondine.* Modena: Arti Grafiche Modenesi, 1952.

Vitti, Antonio. *Giuseppe De Santis and Postwar Italian Cinema.* Toronto: University of Toronto Press, 1996.

Wicke, Jennifer. "Celebrity Material: Materialist Feminism and the Culture of Celebrity." *The South Atlantic Quarterly* 4.93 (1994): 751–778.

Zaniello, Tom. *Working Stiffs, Union Maids, Reds, and Riffraff: An Organized Guide to Films about Labor.* Ithaca, NY: Cornell University Press, 1996.

Zavella, Patricia. *Women's Work and Chicano Families: Cannery Workers of the Santa Clara Valley,* Ithaca: NY, Cornell University Press, 1987.

Zappi, Elda Gentili. *If Eight Hours Seem Too Few: Mobilization of Women Workers in the Italian Rice Fields.* Albany, NY: State University of New York Press, 1991.

Zinn, Dorothy Louise. "Adriatic Brethren or Black Sheep? Migration in Italy and the Albanian Crisis, 1991." *European Urban and Regional Studies* 3.3 (1996): 241–249.

Selected Films

Antonioni, Michelangelo, dir. *Le amiche.* 1955.
Amelio, Gianni, dir. *Lamerica,* 1994.
Coppola, Francis Ford, dir. *The Godfather.* 1972.
———. *The Godfather: Part II.* 1974.
———. *The Godfather: Part III.* 1990.
de Michiel, Helen, dir. *Tarantella.* 1996.
De Santis, Giuseppe, dir. *Riso amaro.* 1949.

De Sica, Vittorio, dir. *Umberto D.* 1952.
Fofi, Gofreddo, dir. *Vesna va veloce.* 1996.
Le Roy, Mervyn, dir. *Little Caesar.* 1930.
Savoca, Nancy, dir. *Household Saints.* 1993.
———. *True Love.* 1989.
Scorsese, Martin, dir. *Goodfellas.* 1990.
———. *Italianamerican,* 1974.
Wellman, William, dir. *Westward the Women.* 1951.

Index

abortion, 60, 61, 62–63
AFL Cannery Workers Union, 109, 111nn9–10
Africa, 19, 73n11
L'Agnese va a morire (Viganò), 39, 46nn18–19, 73n7
agricultural labor, 4, 24–25n4, 33–34, 35, 45n5. *See also mondine*
Albania, 19
Alberti, Margherita Di Fazio, 53–54
Alle risaiole, 43
American Federation of Labor Cannery Workers Union, 109, 111nn9–10
Le amiche, 1–2
"Among Women Alone" (Pavese), 1
Andiamo a spasso (Viarengo), 74n14
anti-Fascism, 15, 36
Antonioni, Michelangelo, 1–2
Arbizzani, Luigi, 36
Are Italians White? (Guglielmo and Salerno), 83
Argentina, 19
Aristarco, Guido, 42
Asia, 73n11
assimilation: and detachment from past

alliances, 105, 106, 109; in *The Godfather*, 78; in *Household Saints*, 92, 93–94, 95, 96–97; of Italian American immigrants, 83–84, 98–99n11, 98n9, 104; in *Tarantella*, 89, 91; in *Westward the Women*, 107
Australia, 19

Baker, Aaron, 92, 93, 94, 95
Bakhtin, Mikhail, 16–17, 28n23, 28n25
Barbieri, Remigio, 45n10
Baron, Ava, 5, 6
Bella ciao, 38, 46n17
Birnbaum, Lucia Chiavola, 8–9, 36, 73n10
Bitter Rice, 37, 42–43, 47n27
Blood Brothers, 82
Bolivia, 19, 64
Bona, Mary Jo, 79
Bono, Paolo, 62
Bortolotti, Franca Pieroni, 45n7
Bossi, Umberto, 74n13
Bound by Distance (Verdicchio), 18, 20
Braidotti, Rosi, 21, 29n31

Index

Brazil, 19
A Bronx Tale, 82

California: cannery workers in, 102, 103, 104–5, 108–9; immigrants from northern Italy in, 111n7; immigrants relocation to, for agricultural employment, 107–8. *See also* San Diego
Calvino, Italo, 42, 47n24, 47n28
Canada, 19
Candelora, Giorgio, 24–25n4
Cannery and Agricultural Workers Industrial Union, 109
cannery workers, 102–3, 104–5, 108–10
Cape Verde, 19
capitalism, 4, 12–13, 54
Capra, Frank, 107
Carlini, Giuliano, 52, 65–67, 69, 70, 74n16
Casalinghe di riserva (Turrini), 63–64
Castellani, Giuliana, 20
Centro Italiano femminile, 73n10
Cgil (Italian General Confederation of Labor), 31–32, 44–45n1, 74n16
Chase, David, 85
China, 19
Chohra, Nassera, 74n14
Christian Democratic Party (DC), 73n10
Cialente, Fausta, 37
Clark, Donald Martin, 29n29
Clark, Martin, 28n26
class: effect on acceptance of immigrants, 3; privileging of, over race in labor histories, 4, 7; relationship to language, 16–17, 28n23
Codrignani, Giancarla, 62
Cohen, Miriam, 25n4, 81
Colombi, Marchesa, 36–37, 43, 44, 46n14, 47n28

common sense: as the basis for cultural identity, 14; emphasis of, in *Household Saints*, 92, 93, 95; folklore *versus*, 27n18; good sense *versus*, 14, 101; role in creating a counter-hegemony, 14–15, 98n6, 101. *See also* folklore
Confetti for Gino (Madalena), 111n3
Cookbook of Happiness (Petronius), 49, 52, 55–57, 72n4
Coppola, Francis Ford, 78, 84–88, 99n14, 99n17, 100n22
Cornelisen, Ann, 45n8
Coro delle mondine, 32, 37–38, 44
counter-hegemony: common sense and, 14–15, 98n6, 101; definition of, 26n15; everyday experiences and, 13, 14, 24, 102, 110, 115; folklore and, 15, 44, 52, 110; language and, 16–17, 28n23; organic intellectuals and, 110; subalterns and, 16, 17, 28n23, 52, 57, 110, 115
Crisantino, Amelia, 52, 65–69, 71–72, 74n16
cryptoethnic, as a term, 98n2
culture. *See* counter-hegemony; international popular culture; national popular culture

Daffini, Giovanna, 46n17
Davis, John A., 25n4
De Grazia, Victoria, 35–36
de Lauretis, Teresa, 9, 10, 79
de Michiel, Helen, 78–79, 88–92, 97, 100n22
Demme, Jonathan, 85, 100n23
DePalma, Brian, 84
De Santis, Giuseppe, 37, 42–43, 47n27
De Sica, Vittorio, 58
di Leonardo, Micaela, 80
Diotima Community, 50
Dirt in the Face (Carlini), 52, 65–67, 69, 70, 74n16

Di Scala, Spencer M., 18–19, 25n4
discrimination. See racism
Distributive, Processing, and Office Workers of America, 108–9
domestic labor: absence of, from labor histories, 4; as gendered labor, 4, 53, 54; low monetary and symbolic value give to, 50; as one of few types of employment open to women immigrants, 19, 23, 64, 71. See also unwaged domestic labor
domestic workers: immigrant women as, and the entrance of middle-class Italian-born women into professional careers, 71–72; influence on the creation of culture, 15, 50–53, 71; isolation of, 49–50; lack of private space allotted to, 59; low value given to the labor of, 70; marginalization of, within publications, 64–65; migration and, 54; occupation of private and public space, 52, 55, 56–57, 70–71; use of creative representations as acts of liberation, 50; women of color as, 23, 29n33, 63–64
Le donne di casa Gramsci (Paulesu), 10

Egypt, 19
emigration from Italy, 18–19, 22, 28n26, 98n4, 111n7
Empire (Hardt and Negri), 24n3
Eritrea, 19
Ethiopia, 19
ethnicity, role of, 4, 6, 7, 103, 105–6, 110
Ets, Marie Hall, 98n5
everyday experiences: in Household Saints, 78; role in the creation of a counter-hegemony, 13, 14, 24, 102, 110, 115; in Tarantella, 78, 89, 90, 91, 92
Ewen, Elizabeth, 7

extracomunitari, 19, 29n28, 74n12. See also immigrants

Fascism, labor protests against, 15, 36
Fatalità (Negri), 37
female rice workers. See mondine
Filipino American cannery workers, 108
folklore, 15, 27n18, 44, 52, 110, 115. See also common sense
food in Italian American cinema, 77, 86–87, 88, 90, 91, 99n15
Fordism, 12, 13, 51
Forgacs, David, 27n20
The Fortunate Pilgrim (Puzo), 88
Forty Days, Forty Nights (Lajolo), 37
France, 5
Fraser, Nancy, 57
From Wiseguys to Wise Men (Gardaphè), 98n3

gangster films: absence of women's labor in, 78, 86, 87; gangsters as Italian American in, 99n16; male bonding in, 99n17; representation of gangsters as cooks in, 77, 78–79, 86–87; rhetoric of nostalgia and, 77–78, 82, 84, 88
Gardaphè, Fred L., 88, 98n3
Gardiner, Michael, 28n23
Gedaf, Irene, 29n31
Ghana, 19, 64
Gilbert, Sandra Mortola, 77
Ginzburg, Natalia, 47n28, 58
Girlfriends, 1–2
Giuseppe De Santis (Vitti), 42
Gluck, Sherna Berger, 5
The Godfather, 78, 84–88, 99n14, 99n17, 100n22
Goodfellas, 77, 86–87, 88, 99n15
good sense, 14, 81, 93, 101
Gramsci, Antonio: as cofounder of the Italian Communist Party and L'Unità, 8; on common sense, 14,

98n6, 101; correspondence with his wife and sister-in-law, 10–11, 12; death of, 8; desire for a new kind of masculine and feminine character, 11–13; discussion of Fordism, 12, 13, 51; education of, 8; on everyday experiences, 13, 14, 102, 110, 155; on folklore, 15, 44, 52, 110, 115; on good sense, 14, 101; imprisonment of, 8, 10; influence of the Gramsci sisters on, 10; involvement in the Italian Socialist Party, 8; on language, 16, 17, 28n23; *Letters from Prison*, 8; on national popular, 15, 27n22; omission of female migrant labor from alliance-making process, 9; on organic intellectuals, 16, 17, 101, 110, 114–15; *Prison Notebooks*, 8, 11, 12; on sexuality in the production of capital and culture, 9, 50; *The Southern Question*, 9, 20, 101, 114; use of the term "war of position," 27n20; view of women, 11. *See also* counter-hegemony, national popular culture, subalterns

Gramsci and Italy's Passive Revolution (Davis), 25n4

Gramsci Notwithstanding, 10

Green, Nancy L., 79

Greenberg, Jaclyn, 108

Gualandi, Irea, 35, 36, 38, 45n6

Guglielmo, Jennifer, 83–84, 105

Guglielmo, Thomas A., 98–99n11

Gutman, Herbert, 7

Habermas, Jurgen, 57

Hall, Stuart, 27n20

Hardt, Michael, 24n3

hegemony. *See* counter-hegemony

Holub, Renate, 9, 10, 13, 17

homosexuality, 26n14

Ho trovato l'occidente (Crisantino), 52, 65–69, 71–72, 74n16

Household Saints, 78–79, 92–97, 100n24, 100n25

Houston, John, 85

How Fascism Ruled Women (De Grazia), 35–36

Hutcheon, Linda, 97–98n2

If Eight Hours Seem Too Few (Zappi), 33

immigrants: acceptance of, 3; exclusion and isolation of, 66–67, 70–71; racism against, 22, 67–69, 71–72; as workers in California's agricultural industry, 105, 107–8, 111n7. *See also* immigrant women, Italian American immigrants, Italian American women

immigrant women: autobiographical narratives of, 65–66; as cannery workers, 102–3, 104, 110; creation of an international popular culture, 69–70, 72; lack of cross-immigrant alliances between, 67, 69, 71; racism against, 22, 67–69, 71–72; rearticulation of racist discourse of the dominant culture, 67–68; types of employment open to, 19, 23, 64, 71. *See also* domestic workers, Italian American women

Immigrant Women in the Land of Dollars (Ewen), 7

immigration to Italy, 19, 28–29n28, 29n29, 64, 73n11

In risaia (Colombi), 36–37, 43, 44, 46n14

international popular culture, 18, 53, 69–70, 72, 92

In the Rice Field (book: Colombi), 36–37, 43, 44, 46n14

In the Rice Fields (pamphlet), 43

I promessi sposi (Manzoni), 54

Iran, 19

Italianamerican, 99n15

Italian American immigrants: cinematic representations of, and the rhetoric

of nostalgia, 79–84. *See also* Italian American women
Italian American immigrants and whiteness. *See* assimilation of Italian American immigrants
Italian American women: assimilation into mainstream dominant culture, 98n9; as cannery workers, 104–5; changing roles of, 83, 98n9; cinematic portrayal of, as outside of labor, 78, 80–81, 82, 84, 88; in *Household Saints*, 78–79, 92–97; lack of historical information about labor contributions of, 79–80; in *Tarantella*, 78–79, 88–89, 90–91, 97. *See also* Italian American immigrants
Italian General Confederation of Labor (Cgil), 31–32, 44–45n1, 74n16
Italian rice workers. *See mondine*
Italian Socialist Party (PSI): formation of, 33; membership, 8, 41, 43; position on abortion, 61, 62; representation of, in *Una storia di ragazze*, 63; women's leagues organized by, 34, 45n7
Italy: constitution of, 2; emigration from, 18–19, 22, 28n26, 98n4, 111n7; entrance of middle-class Italian-born women into professional careers, 71–72; exclusion and isolation of immigrants to, from middle-class identity, 66–67, 70–71; immigration to, 19, 28–29n28, 29n29, 64, 73n11; internal migration in, 19, 22, 28n27, 33–34, 36, 74n13; legalization of abortion, 60; marginal status of women in the dominant culture of, 65; as outside the borders of the first world, 3, 24n3; as predominantly peasant-based at the end of World War II, 24n3; racism against immigrants in, 22, 67–69, 71–72; racism against southern Italians by northern Italians, 19, 22, 74n13; women's right to vote in, 5, 46n22, 73n10. *See also* domestic labor, domestic workers, *mondine*
I've Discovered the West (Crisantino), 52, 65–69, 71–72, 74n16

Japanese American cannery workers, 104, 108
Jewish immigrant women, 7

Kemp, Sandra, 62
Krieger, Bob, 22, 29n32
Kroha, Lucienne, 43–44, 47n28

labor histories: absence of women from, 4–6, 7, 110; exclusion of agricultural labor from, 4, 24–25n4, 33–34, 35, 45n5; lack of discussion about domestic labor in, 4; lack of recognition of the roles of race and ethnicity by, 4, 6, 7, 105–6; marginal status of cannery workers within, 102–3; revisionist approaches to, 4–5
labor protests, 9, 15, 26n10, 31, 33, 34–36
Lajolo, Davide, 37, 42
Lakhous, Amara, 74n14
Landy, Marcia, 9, 12, 13, 14–15, 52–53
Latino cannery workers, 103, 104, 106
Leaving Little Italy (Gardaphè), 88
Le mondine (Viganò), 37, 46n13
LeRoy, Mervyn, 99n16
Letters from Prison (Gramsci), 8
Liberazione delle donne (Birnbaum), 36
Little Caesar, 99n16
Lollobrigida, Gina, 22
Loren, Sofia, 22
Lowe, Lisa, 15, 65

Mac, 82
Madalena, Lorenzo, 111n3
"Mafioso" (Gilbert), 77

magical realism, 95
Maid in the U.S.A. (Romero), 23
Mangano, Silvana, 22, 42, 43
Mangione, Jerre, 80, 83
Manzoni, Alessandro, 54
Margotti, Maria: death of, 31–32, 41, 43, 44–45n1; as a historical figure, 38–39, 41, 42
marionettes, 90
Martinez, Thomas, 102, 103, 104, 106, 108, 110
Marxism, 4, 7
Mazza, Maria, 22, 23
Mechling, Jay, 107
Meluschi, Antonio, 38, 40–41
Mendez, Denny, 22, 23, 29n32
Mexican American cannery workers, 103, 104, 106, 108
Middle East, 73n11
migration. *See* emigration from Italy; immigration to Italy
Mirigliani, Enzo, 22
Miss Italia pageant of 1996, 22, 23
mobster films. *See* gangster films
Modern Italy (Clark), 28n26
Modotti, Tina, 14, 24, 113–14, 115
Mohanty, Chandra Talpade, 7, 25n6
Mondariso, 38
mondine: creative and critical texts about, 36–37, 39–40, 42, 43; definition of, 44n2; diversity among, 34, 35; formation of a counter-hegemonic national popular culture, 32–33, 37–39, 41–42, 44; lack of coverage in labor histories about, 33–34, 35, 45n5; organized group protests of, 9, 26n10, 31, 33, 34–36; paintings and photographs of, 37, 46n13; as seasonal migrants, 33–34, 36; symbolic link to all underrepresented people, 32, 41–42, 43; tradition of singing, 15, 32, 37–38. *See also* Margotti, Maria

Le mondine (Viganò), 37, 39–40, 41, 46n13
Montanari, Otto, 33–34, 35
Morocco, 19
Morreale, Ben, 80, 83
motherhood, unwed, 14, 60, 61–62, 63, 73n9
Murphy, Timothy S., 18
Mussolini, Benito, 8, 26n14, 35, 36

national popular, 15, 27n22
national popular culture: dependency on language, 16–18, 28n23; establishment of a, in *Tarantella*, 79, 89, 90, 91, 92; participation of the mondine in the formation of, 32–33, 37–39, 41–42, 44; potential of domestic workers to create a, 51, 52–53, 71; production of, by subaltern classes, 8, 14, 15–16, 50, 81, 110; representations of the operations of, in *Household Saints*, 97; use of visual representations to create, 102, 105, 106
Negri, Ada, 37, 46n12
Negri, Antonio, 24n3
Noce, Teresa, 36
Noi donne, 37, 38, 58
Nomadic Subjects (Braidotti), 21
nomadism, 21, 29n31
Nonostante Gramsci, 10
nostalgia, rhetoric of, 79–84, 86, 88, 89, 90–91

oral narratives, 20, 65, 69–70, 72
organic intellectuals: in *Household Saints*, 79; role in the development of an alternative national popular culture, 16, 17, 101, 110, 114–15; in *Tarantella*, 79, 89, 90, 91, 92

Palazzi, Maura, 54, 72
Parati, Graziella, 74n14

Paterlini, Marco, 33, 45n6
Paulesu, Mimma, 10
Pavese, Cesare, 1
Petronius, 49, 52
Philippines, 19
photographs: as a political tool, 113, 114, 115; use of, to create a national popular culture, 102, 105, 106
Picarazzi, Teresa, 20, 66, 74n17
Pileggi, Nicholas, 86, 97n1
Portuguese American cannery workers, 104, 108
Prison Notebooks (Gramsci), 8, 11, 12
private spaces and public spaces: domestic workers inhabitation of, 52, 55, 56–57, 70–71; Household Saints' critique of, 92, 93–94; relationship between, 14, 89, 114
PSI. *See* Italian Socialist Party (PSI)
Pucci, Idanna, 98n5
Puzo, Mario, 84, 88

Quaderni dal carcere (Gramsci), 8, 11, 12
Quando saremo a Reggio Emilia (Paterlini), 33, 45n6
Quaranta giorni, quaranta notti (Lajolo), 37
Quasi, Annarella, 45n10

race: effect on acceptance of immigrants, 3; effect on internal migration within postwar Italy, 3; lack of recognition of the role of, by labor histories, 4, 6, 7, 105–6
racism: against immigrants in Italy, 22, 67–69, 71–72; rearticulation of dominant culture's discourse of, by minority classes, 67–68; against southern Italians by northern Italians, 19, 22, 74n13
Ready-to-Wear and Ready-to-Work (Green), 79

Red Week, 9, 26n10
Reich, Jacqueline, 82, 97
rhetoric of nostalgia, 79–84, 86, 88, 89, 90–91
Riccettario della felicità (Petronius), 49, 52, 55–57, 72n4
Riccò, Gianfranco, 33–34, 35
rice workers. *See mondine*
Riso amaro, 37, 42–43, 47n27
Rivolta femminile group, 8–9
Roediger, David R., 4, 7, 26n9, 105, 109, 110
Romania, 19
Romero, Mary, 23, 52, 59
Rosa, the Life of an Italian Immigrant (Ets), 98n5
Rosie the Riveter Revisited (Gluck), 5

Salerno, Salvatore, 83–84
San Diego, 103–4, 106. *See also* California
Sarti, Raffaella, 53
Sasson, Anne Showstack, 9, 13, 14, 27n20
Sautman, Francesca Canadé, 82, 87
Savoca, Nancy, 78–79, 92–97, 100nn23–25
Scansance, Vasco, 46n17
Schucht, Julia, 10, 12
Schucht, Tatiana, 10
Scontro di civiltà per un ascensore a piazza Vittorio (Lakhous), 74n14
Scorsese, Catherine, 99n15
Scorsese, Martin, 77, 84, 86–87, 88, 99n15
Scott, Joan, 1, 4–5, 6
Senegal, 19
sexuality, role of, 4, 9, 11–13, 50, 51
single motherhood, 14, 60, 61–62, 63, 73n9
Socialismo e questione femminile (Bortolotti), 45n7
Soja, Edward, 87–88, 99n18

The Sopranos, 85
The Southern Question (Gramsci), 9, 20, 101, 114
speech genres, 16, 17, 28n24
Sraffa, Piero, 10
Sri Lanka, 19
Stam, Robert, 80
Starr, Kevin, 109
States of Grace (Clark), 29n29
stereotypes of Italian Americans, 82–83, 84, 89, 90–91
Storia dell'Italia moderna (Candelora), 24–25n4
Una storia di ragazze (Viganò), 14, 52, 58–63
La Storia (Mangione and Morreale), 80
Le storiche, 6
A Story about Girls (Viganò), 14, 52, 58–63
subalterns: ability to create a counter-hegemony, 16, 17, 28n23, 52, 57, 110, 115; alliances between, 24, 39, 102; definition of, 8; relationship between organic intellectuals and, 114–15; role in developing a national popular culture, 8, 14, 15–16, 50, 81, 110

Tarantella, 78–79, 88–92, 97, 100n22
La terra in faccia (Carlini), 52, 65–67, 69, 70, 74n16
testimonials of immigrant women, 20, 65, 69–70, 72
thirdspace, 87–88, 99n18
Ti ho sposato per allegria (Ginzburg), 58
Tommasi, Wanda, 50–51, 72n1
Tra cronaca, storia, e testimonianza (Gualandi), 45n6
"Tra donne sole" (Pavese), 1
The Trials of Maria Barbella (Pucci), 98n5
True Love, 100n23

Tunisia, 19
Turrini, Olda, 63–64

UDI (Unione donne italiane), 62, 73n10
Ukraine, 19, 64
Umberto D., 58
"Under Western Eyes" (Mohanty), 7
Unione donne italiane (UDI), 62, 73n10
unions, 108–9, 111nn9–10
L'Unità, 8, 37, 39
United States: domestic labor in, 23; immigration to, from Italy, 19, 28–29n28, 98n4, 111n7. *See also* California, Italian American immigrants, Italian American women, San Diego
unwaged domestic labor: in *Household Saints*, 95; in *Tarantella*, 89, 91
unwed motherhood, 14, 60, 61–62, 63, 73n9

Verdicchio, Pasquale, 18, 20, 104, 113, 114
"Viaggio in risaia" (Cialente), 37
Viarengo, Maria, 74n14
Viganò, Renata: *L'Agnese va a morire*, 39, 46nn18–19, 73n7; creation of Margotti as a historical figure, 38–39, 41, 42; linking of the mondine to all underrepresented people, 41–42, 43; *Le mondine*, 37, 39–40, 41, 46n13; personal history and political activism of, 39–41, 58, 72–73n5; on single motherhood, 73n9; *Una storia di ragazze*, 14, 52, 58–63; writing of, as part of a national popular culture, 33, 44
Vitti, Antonio, 42
Vitullo, Julian, 92, 93, 94, 95
Volevo diventare bianca (Chohra), 74n14
"Voyage in the Rice Fields" (Cialente), 37

Wages of Whiteness (Roediger), 4, 7, 105
war of position, 27n20
Wellman, William, 102, 107–9
Weston, Edward, 113
Westward the Women, 102, 107–9
White on Arrival (Guglielmo), 98–99n11
wiseguy. *See* gangster films
Wiseguy (Pileggi), 86, 97n1
women: absence of, from labor histories, 4–6, 7, 110; of color as domestic workers, 23, 29n33, 63–64; Gramsci's description of a new type of, 11–12; immigration to Italy, 19; independence of wives of migrating men, 34, 45n8; labor as a mode of expression and independence for, 1–2; limitations on involvement of, in labor protests, 34; marginal status of, in dominant Italian culture, 65; right to vote, 5, 46n22, 73n10; role in the formation of culture as subalterns, 8–9. *See also* domestic workers, immigrant women, Italian American women, *mondine*
The Women of Gramsci's Home (Paulesu), 10
women rice workers. *See mondine*
The Women Rice Workers (Viganò), 37, 39–40, 41, 46n13
The Women Writer in Late Nineteenth Century Italy, 43–44
Work Engendered (Baron), 5
working classes. *See* subalterns
Workshop to Office (Cohen), 25n4, 81
World War II, 5, 35–36, 38, 41

Zappi, Elda Gentili, 9, 33, 34, 35, 45n6

About the Author

Laura E. Ruberto, Ph.D. (University of California at San Diego, 1999) is currently a professor in the department of arts and humanities at Berkeley City College in California. Her coedited collections include *Italian Neorealism and Global Cinema* (2007) and *Bakhtin and the Nation* (1999). She has also been a special editor to the *Journal of the West* (Fall 2004). In 2006 she received a Junior Faculty Fulbright Research Award to Italy.